Great Loves

Great Loves

Produced for DK by Toucan Books

DK LONDON
Senior Editor Victoria Heyworth-Dunne
Senior Designer Mark Cavanagh
Managing Editor Gareth Jones
Senior Managing Art Editor Lee Griffiths
Senior Production Editor Andy Hilliard
Senior Production Controller Rachel Ng
Illustrator Emma Fraser Reid
Jacket Design Development Manager
Sophia M.T.T.
Jacket Designer Akiko Kato
Associate Publishing Director Liz Wheeler
Art Director Karen Self
Publishing Director Jonathan Metcalf

First American Edition, 2022
Published in the United States by DK Publishing
1450 Broadway, Suite 801, New York, NY 10018

A catalog record for this book
is available from the Library of Congress.
ISBN: 978-0-7440-5027-1

Printed and bound in China

For the curious
www.dk.com

FSC
www.fsc.org
MIX
Paper from
responsible sources
FSC™ C018179

This book was made with Forest
Stewardship Council™ certified
paper—one small step in DK's
commitment to a sustainable future.
For more information go to
www.dk.com/our-green-pledge

Contents

Tragic love

Kindred spirits

Enduring love

Introduction

Love makes the world go round, but it also hurts, and "the course of true love never did run smooth," as Lysander observes in Shakespeare's *A Midsummer Night's Dream*. While universally yearned for, great love is not easy to find or keep. It is therefore more precious and more envied than money, power, or fame.

This book celebrates history's greatest loves from ancient times to the current day. There are betrothals and betrayals, passion and pathos, wooings and weddings, as well as *coups de foudre* and slow burns that build over time. From the tragic tale of Antony and Cleopatra, to the tempestuous marriage of Frida Kahlo and Diego Rivera, to the enduring contentment of the Ladies of Llangollen, love has as many faces as there are lovers.

There are kindred spirits who seem to be meant for each other, and lovers whom fate or families conspire to keep apart. Some couples have shared historic moments of triumph or tragedy; others have fought injustice side by side, founding nations and changing the world. Some great loves have ended in death and destruction, and others have proved eternal. Rulers such as Shah Jahan and Queen Victoria have immortalized their beloveds in stone, while artists, singers, and writers have poured their hearts onto paper or sung their love's praises to the heavens. These remarkable love stories, be they unforgettable, forbidden, tragic, or enduring, show the true power of love.

Unforgettable
love

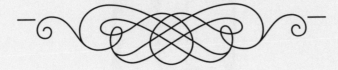

Nefertari

◇

Ramses II

The pharaoh's favorite queen

C. 1279–1250 BCE

Over his 66-year reign, Ramses II, known as Ramses the Great, had at least eight wives and fathered as many as 100 children with his wives and concubines. Yet it is the pharaoh's love for his first wife, Nefertari, that history remembers.

The grandson of Ramses I—the founder of Ancient Egypt's 19th dynasty—Ramses II was introduced to his royal duties at a young age. Before becoming king in 1279 BCE, the adolescent Ramses married Nefertari, a girl in her teens, probably from a noble family in Thebes (today's Luxor). Although Ramses married another wife at around the same time, Nefertari was always the future pharaoh's chief wife and his favorite. Her name means "beautiful companion."

Nefertari acquired the title "Mother of the King" when she gave birth to Ramses' first son. In fact, Prince Amun-her-khepeshef died as a young man, and although Ramses and Nefertari had many children together, none of Nefertari's sons outlived their father to ascend the throne.

" For Nefertari ... for whom the sun doth shine. "

Inscription, Small Temple, Abu Simbel

In the early years of their marriage, Nefertari participated in state affairs, accompanying her husband on state occasions and traveling with him through the kingdom. Her important role is reflected in the number of monuments bearing her image with her signature vulture headdress. Throughout her life, Nefertari also received royal titles from her husband, including "Great of Favors" and "God's Wife."

Nefertari died in her mid-40s, around 1250 BCE, the cause of her death unknown. The pharaoh paid tribute to his first wife with an elaborate tomb in the Valley of the Queens, in Thebes, and in a rock-cut temple at Abu Simbel, where she is uniquely represented at the same size as Ramses himself. In the years after Nefertari's death, Ramses continued to have statues of his late wife erected throughout his kingdom.

Alexander
—◇—
Hephaestion

A king and his general

c. 343–324 BCE

The most important person in Alexander the Great's life was his beloved general Hephaestion. The son of a Macedonian general, Hephaestion Amyntoros had grown up with Alexander at court. As boys, the two were tutored together by the philosopher Aristotle.

Alexander became king when he was 20 years old. He earned the epithet "the Great" as a military conqueror, with Hephaestion, his boyhood friend, at his side. Hephaestion was once even mistaken for Alexander. The King took no offense, saying that they were both Alexander—a sign of their closeness. The Cynic Epistles, written in the 1st century CE, claim Alexander was "ruled by Hephaestion's thighs."

The king was inspired by Achilles—the legendary hero of the Trojan War. He is said to have laid a wreath at a memorial to Achilles while Hephaestion laid one to Patroclus, Achilles' lover. Like Patroclus, Hephaestion died first, in 324 BCE. Less than a year later, Alexander passed away, at the age of 32. Some said that without Hephaestion, he had lost the will to live.

Dong Xian

Emperor Ai

The passion of the cut sleeve

C. **4–1 BCE**

Dong Xian, originally a minor official in the Han Chinese court, caught the eye of Emperor Ai of Han when he was 19 years old. The emperor (reigned 7–1 BCE) was 23, and had been on the throne for three years. Much to the dismay of the rest of the court—especially his own relatives, who were jockeying for power—Emperor Ai plied Dong Xian and his family with titles, promotions, and grain.

Dong Xian and the emperor were both already married, but their relationship was not considered detrimental to those bonds. The practice of taking a "male favorite" was so common that such lovers were listed in the official records of the Han dynasty.

The relationship between Emperor Ai and Dong Xian was not simply physical. The histories describe an episode when the couple were napping together in the palace in Chang'an, the emperor wearing a traditional imperial robe with long draping sleeves. When the emperor awoke, needing to leave, he found that Dong Xian was lying on one of these sleeves. The emperor loved Dong Xian so much that he cut the sleeve from his own robe rather than wake him.

Sadly, their happiness was short-lived. Emperor Ai died in 1 BCE. On his deathbed, he tried to name Dong Xian as his heir, but the grief-stricken Dong Xian ignored his proclamation. As power passed to the emperor's greedy relatives, Dong Xian, his wife, and the emperor's widow all died by suicide. Despite this unhappy ending, the story of this great romance has endured, with "the passion of the cut sleeve" becoming a euphemism for homosexuality in China.

Beatrice

Dante

The ultimate muse

1275–1290

" From little spark
may burst a mighty flame. **"**

Dante, 1320

Beatrice was Dante's muse. The romance between the Italian poet and the daughter of a Florentine noble family seems to have existed almost entirely in his mind. Their two encounters were fleeting and they never touched. Nonetheless, Beatrice was Dante's saint and guardian angel. Her effect on the poet is chronicled in his poetic development, from *La vita nuova* (*The New Life*) to the Purgatorio and Paradiso sections of *The Divine Comedy*.

Dante first glimpsed Beatrice when she "was at the beginning of her ninth year almost"; he was around the same age. She was dressed in "a restrained crimson," and he was struck by her beauty. The experience was transformational for him. In *La vita nuova*, he recalls his most vital spirit saying, "Behold a god more powerful than I, who, coming, will rule over me."

Their second and last meeting was nine years later, when the pair encountered each other in passing at the "ninth hour of the day." Dante went on to marry someone else in 1285, a match arranged by his parents, as did Beatrice in 1287 (three years before her death), but as a muse and guiding spirit Beatrice's effect on Dante was eternal.

Dante meets Beatrice (in the pale dress) in an 1883 painting by Henry Holiday.

Anne Boleyn

⸻ ✻ ⸻

Henry VIII

The king's obsession

c.1522–1536

The relationship between Henry VIII and Anne Boleyn altered the course of English history. The king was determined to marry the woman he loved in spite of being already married, even if that meant breaking with Roman Catholicism and establishing a new branch of protestantism—the Church of England.

When Henry first met Anne, he was married to his brother's widow, Catherine of Aragon, but their relationship had foundered on their inability to have a male heir who lived beyond infancy. Despite Catherine becoming pregnant six times, she had only a daughter to show for it. The king's patience had worn thin.

Anne Boleyn was probably still a teenager when she arrived at the Tudor court in 1522, having previously been a companion of Henry's sister, Mary, who was married to the French king. Anne captivated the English court with her glamorous French fashions.

> " The longer the days are, the more distant is the sun, and nevertheless the hotter; so is it with our love. "

Henry VIII, c. 1527

How or when she caught Henry's eye is not known for certain, but once Henry had her in his sights, Anne's other suitors fell away. The king stopped a prospective marriage between Anne and Henry Percy, later the Earl of Northumberland.

When Henry asked Anne to become his mistress in around 1526, Anne refused. She may have been influenced by Henry's treatment of her sister, Mary Boleyn, a previous mistress whom he had cast aside with nothing to show for it. Whatever her reasons, Anne told the king, "I would rather lose my life than my honesty." Her reluctance only increased Henry's desire.

Henry was obsessive in his affections. He wrote Anne at least 17 love letters—despite reportedly hating letter writing. She returned his affections by giving him gifts, but was frequently slow to respond to his correspondence. Only one letter Anne sent to the king survives, and its authenticity has been contested by historians. Whether she ever truly returned Henry's love remains a mystery.

By 1527, Henry realized that the only way he could sleep with Anne was by marrying her. The letters between them became more chaste, as he resigned himself to waiting until he was in a position to marry. As a Catholic, Henry was not permitted to divorce his first wife, so he sought an annulment from the Pope, claiming that his marriage to Catherine, his brother Arthur's widow, had contravened God's will. Catherine, who had always maintained that her marriage to the 15-year-old Arthur had not been consummated, disputed this.

In 1531, Henry's request for an annulment was denied, and in accordance with his growing dislike of the power of the Pope, Henry broke away from Rome and its church. In a move that would have far-reaching consequences, Henry created the Church of England under the rule of the king, God's deputy on Earth. He was now able

First Meeting of Henry VIII and Anne Boleyn, by Irish painter Daniel Maclise (1806–1870)

" I hope shortly to make you sing. "

Henry VIII, 1528

to end his first marriage. The annulment was made official in May 1533—after Henry had already married Anne in secret in January. In September of that year, she gave birth to a daughter, Elizabeth.

Like Catherine before her, Anne fell out of favor with Henry after four pregnancies in three years failed to result in a son. As Henry's initial love for his wife turned to anger, his eye began to wander. In early 1536, he set his sights on Jane Seymour—one of Anne's own ladies-in-waiting. Jane, like Anne before her, was unwilling to become the king's mistress and initially refused his lustful advances. As before, this only increased Henry's ardor.

Henry's decision to replace Anne was swift and brutal. On May 2, 1536, Anne was arrested and imprisoned in the Tower of London, accused of adultery, treason, and incest with her brother George. On May 12, she was tried and found guilty of all charges, despite a lack of evidence. Less than a week later, Anne's marriage to Henry was annulled, and her daughter, Elizabeth, declared illegitimate (a move that was later reversed).

On May 19, 1536, just 17 days after her arrest, Anne became the first—but not the last—of Henry's wives to lose her head on Tower Green, with a blow by a French swordsman. Before she was led out on to the scaffold, she swore upon the Holy Sacraments that she had never been unfaithful to the king. Henry did not witness the execution. He became betrothed to Jane Seymour the following day and married her ten days later.

Henry's children

Only three of Henry's legitimate children survived infancy. Edward, conceived with Jane Seymour, succeeded to the throne on Henry's death in 1547, but died six years later, aged just 15. Mary, Henry's daughter with Catherine of Aragon, became the first queen to rule England in 1553, but also died within a few years. In 1558, Elizabeth (left), Henry's daughter with Anne Boleyn, succeeded Mary, beginning a glorious 45-year reign as Queen Elizabeth I.

Tommaso dei Cavalieri

Michelangelo

The adored and the adoring

c.1532–1564

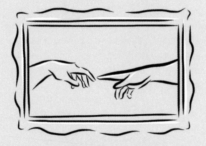

> **❝** I'll forget your name the day I forget the food I live on. **❞**

Michelangelo, 1528

Tommaso may have been the model for Michelangelo's *Head of a Virgin.*

In 1532, Michelangelo met a noble Roman youth named Tommaso dei Cavalieri who would become the great muse of the artist's life, inspiring drawings, letters, and more than 300 poems. Michelangelo was in his late fifties and Tommaso in his late teens or early twenties. Michelangelo gave Tommaso paintings of ancient Greek subjects that celebrated love between an older and a younger man. There is little proof that Tommaso returned the artist's feelings, although they remained close until Michelangelo's death in 1564, with Tommaso by his side. After his death, Tommaso finished Michelangelo's architectural work on the Capitoline Hill.

Historians debate whether the relationship between the artist and his muse was ever sexual. Michelangelo was known for his depictions of the male form as the ideal of beauty—like other artists at the time, he used male models to stand in for women and then added breasts. Homoerotic elements in Michelangelo's art fell prey to censors, and in 1892, a scholar discovered that Michelangelo's great-nephew had changed masculine pronouns to feminine in his poetry—denying the artist's true history to readers for more than 200 years.

Shah Jahan

◇

Mumtaz Mahal

A monument to love

1607–1631

" O Soul, thou art at rest. Return
to the Lord at peace with Him,
and He at peace with you. "

The Quran

An Indian miniature shows the Shah embracing his wife.

Like many great love stories, the tale of Mughal emperor Shah Jahan and his favorite wife, Mumtaz Mahal, was marred by the hard hand of fate. Born of Persian nobility, Mumtaz, whose name means "chosen one of the palace," was beautiful and accomplished, fluent in Arabic and Persian, and skilled at chess. Betrothed at 14, she became Shah Jahan's second wife at the age of 19; he was five years older.

The couple's 19-year marriage was brought to an end in 1631, when Mumtaz died during the birth of their 14th child. Legend says Shah Jahan went gray overnight. In her memory, he employed thousands of craftsmen to fashion a shimmering marble mausoleum for her—the Taj Mahal, a wonder of the modern world.

In 1658, Shah Jahan was overthrown by their son Aurangzeb and imprisoned at Agra Fort, across the Yamuna River from the Taj. It is said that Shah Jahan died gazing over the water. The cenotaphs of Shah Jahan and Mumtaz lie side by side in the Taj, befitting the place they held in each other's heart.

Louis XV

❖ ❖ ❖

Madame de Pompadour

The king and the courtesan

1745–1751

I n 1745, King Louis XV of France hosted a masquerade ball at Versailles, his palace near Paris. Jeanne-Antoinette Poisson was not an aristocrat, but she was sufficiently well-connected to receive an invitation. Intent on making an impression on the king at the ball, she deliberately caught his attention by dropping her handkerchief and then disappearing, a tacit invitation for him to find her. Her ploy was successful. Later that year, the king made Jeanne-Antoinette his official mistress, installing her in an apartment at Versailles, joined to his own by a secret staircase. She was made Marquise de Pompadour with her own grand estate.

Madame de Pompadour, as she became known, was beautiful, intelligent, and cultured. Her brilliant mind earned her great influence and she became Louis XV's closest advisor, said to control all audiences with him. With power, however, came enemies, and critics began to blame her for French misfortunes, such as the country's defeats in the Seven Years' War with Britain and Prussia.

In around 1750, the king's ardor waned. Jeanne-Antoinette's period as Louis' mistress had ended, but her role as his advisor and confidante continued. She took a particular interest in the arts and new construction projects. The Place de la Concorde in Paris and Petit Trianon at Versailles were built in part thanks to her patronage. Her influence and friendship with the king would last until 1764, when she died of tuberculosis at the age of 42. Madame de Pompadour took her last breath at Versailles, where it all began.

" The handkerchief is thrown. "

Murmur in the gallery of the court, 1745

Joséphine

—◇—

Napoleon

War and peace

1796–1809

The French Revolution brought Napoleon Bonaparte and Joséphine de Beauharnais together, but Napoleon's rise from an ambitious army officer to the first emperor of France would eventually tear them apart. When Napoleon met Joséphine in 1795, she was the widow of Alexandre de Beauharnais, a French nobleman and revolutionary who had been executed during the Reign of Terror (September 1793–July 1794), when many people suspected of being enemies of the French Revolution were murdered. Joséphine only escaped the guillotine because the leader of the Reign of Terror was guillotined the day before her own execution was scheduled.

While Joséphine was a widow looking for a patron, Napoleon was a rising military star who was looking for a well-to-do wife. Despite these pragmatic reasons for beginning a relationship, Napoleon seems to have genuinely fallen in love with Joséphine, and proposed to her in January 1796. His family disapproved—both because of Joséphine's age (she was 32, 6 years his senior) and the fact that she was a widow with two children. Napoleon cared about neither, but Joséphine was initially hesitant to accept his proposal, finding him awkward and strange. Nonetheless, the pair were married two months later.

Napoleon left for a military campaign days after the wedding, having been named commander-in-chief of the army fighting in Italy. The new general kept in touch with his beloved wife with a series of

> " A kiss on your heart, and one
> much lower down, much lower! "
>
> **Napoleon Bonaparte**, 1796

impassioned letters that reveal the ups and downs in their marriage. Napoleon's letters became more ardent as rumors of his wife's infidelity began to circulate. Although Napoleon was also deceiving Joséphine, he did not believe she was unfaithful to him until he visited her apartment in Milan and found her missing. After more than a week of waiting, he wrote Joséphine a furious letter full of accusations, leading her to blame his family for conspiring against her. This episode was a turning point in their relationship—Joséphine became more outwardly loving toward him, and Napoleon more suspicious.

In 1798, Napoleon took a mistress whom he met while campaigning in Egypt—Pauline Fourès, the wife of one of his officers. The following year, the affair led to public embarrassment for Joséphine when the British intercepted and published the contents of a letter in which Napoleon complained about the state of his marriage. After a stormy confrontation on Napoleon's return to France, he and Joséphine reconciled: she agreed that she would never again be unfaithful, a vow she kept; Napoleon made no such promise, because, he claimed, his mistresses did not arouse his heart—and therefore did not count.

When Napoleon became Emperor in 1804, he named Joséphine Empress of the French Empire. At this point, the pair had been married for eight years, much of which Napoleon had spent away on campaigns. Now, however, Napoleon began to think about his legacy. Joséphine had children by her first husband, but she and Napoleon found themselves unable to have a child together. Joséphine had tried treatments for her apparent infertility but without success. The failure to produce an heir spelled the end of their marriage. In 1806, one of Napoleon's mistresses gave birth to a child, and he began to consider the ramifications of Joséphine's infertility. Having an heir was paramount to securing the longevity of his empire, and with a heavy heart he had the marriage annulled in 1810 on the grounds that a parish priest had not been present at the wedding.

Napoleon had married Joséphine for love but had divorced her for politics. His heart was still hers, and he famously wrote of his new wife Marie Louise of Austria, "I have married a womb." After their divorce, Joséphine retained her title of empress, and was given the estate of Malmaison, near Paris. She and Napoleon continued to correspond, and he occasionally visited her. Joséphine died of pneumonia at Malmaison in May 1814, 26 days after her former husband's exile to the island of Elba following his defeat by the British at the Battle of Waterloo.

Roses for a Rose

Joséphine was Napoleon's name for his wife. She had previously used the name Rose, from her given name of Marie Josèphe-Rose. The empress was fond of her old namesake, and between 1804 and 1814 built up the world's largest rose collection. Ever supportive of his wife's hobby, Napoleon encouraged the French Navy to bring back rose seeds from foreign lands and even permitted ships carrying specimens from British nurseries to pass through his naval blockade.

Napoleon and Joséphine, *c.* 1800

" I ask of you neither eternal love,
nor fidelity, but simply ... truth. "

Napoleon, 1796

Lady Hamilton

·———◆———·

Lord Nelson

The sea dog and the femme fatale

1798–1805

" I never will retract one syllable
I uttered, or one thought I felt. "

Admiral Nelson, 1802

Emma Hamilton and Admiral Nelson

Few were impervious to Lady Emma Hamilton's charms. The British portrait artist George Romney frequently painted her, and the King and Queen of Naples were her confidantes, a fact that persuaded the elderly British minister to Naples, Sir William Hamilton, to marry her. When 39-year-old Rear Admiral Horatio Nelson, the most daring and accomplished officer in Britain's Royal Navy, sailed into the Neapolitan harbor in July 1798, the die was cast.

Nelson, who was also married, became infatuated with Emma. Their affair scandalized London, where they lived openly with their illegitimate daughter Horatia, born in 1801. Eventually duty called, and at the climax of his greatest victory, the Battle of Trafalgar in 1805, Nelson was cut down by a bullet that severed his spine.

Emma Hamilton carried on for years without Nelson, living in style while disguising her declining fortunes. Eventually, she fell into oblivion, landing in debtors' prison before dying in Calais in 1815, buried in a pauper's grave.

Peter Doyle

•———◆———•

Walt Whitman

From chance encounter to a seven-year romance

c. 1865–1880s

66 We were familiar at once—I put my hand on his knee—we understood ... from that moment on we were the biggest sort of friends. **99**

Peter Doyle, 1895

Walt Whitman (left) and Peter Doyle, c. 1865

American poet Walt Whitman met Peter Doyle on a stormy evening in 1865. Whitman was on his way home from a meeting with fellow writer John Borroughs, and was the only passenger on a Washington, D.C., streetcar. The conductor of the car was Peter, who, in view of the weather and the lack of passengers, decided to keep Walt company. The two looked at each other, Peter boldly put a hand on Walt's knee, and Walt stayed on the car when it reached his stop. That night, Walt went home with Peter.

The two were opposites—Walt was a 45-year-old established poet, and a staunch Unionist; Peter was a poorly educated 21-year-old Confederate veteran. Yet for seven years Peter was Walt's muse. The main character in the poem "Come Up From The Fields Father" was named after him. When Walt had a stroke in 1873, Peter helped take care of him, but the relationship began to decline when Walt moved to Camden, New Jersey, in 1873. Apart from a few meetings in the 1880s, the relationship dwindled to an infrequent correspondence.

Mercedes de Acosta

◊

Greta Garbo

Behind the screen
1931–1941

The relationship between Swedish actor Greta Garbo and Cuban-American writer Mercedes de Acosta is full of intrigue. Although Greta's estate maintains to this day that the relationship was platonic, Mercedes' memoir *Here Lies the Heart*, published in 1960, suggests otherwise, and includes a picture of Greta sunbathing topless.

Greta and Mercedes exchanged letters for decades—from 1931, when they first met in Santa Monica, California, introduced by the screenwriter Salka Viertel, until 1958. In 1931, Greta was already a famous silent film star in Hollywood, with 15 films to her name since signing a contract with Metro-Goldwyn-Mayer in 1925. Mercedes was a social dynamo, in elite circles as well as in drag clubs and speakeasies, and was described as "a woman with a passionate and intense devotion to the art of living." Although Mercedes was married to portrait painter Abram Poole from 1920 to 1935, she was openly lesbian, and surrounded herself with interesting and beautiful women with whom she had affairs. Mercedes claimed to have had romantic relationships with dancer Isadora Duncan and actor Marlene Dietrich, Greta's Hollywood rival.

Both Mercedes and Greta loved tailored suits, giving them an androgynous air. Mercedes almost always dressed in black or white and rejected constraining female fashion; Greta liked trousers and set a new trend for them in the film *The Single Standard* (1929), in which she wears the jackets and trousers of her on-screen lover. In later life, Mercedes wore a patch over one eye,

> **"** I knew this would happen between you and me. I knew it from your walk, your look, your opening of the door. **"**

Mercedes de Acosta

for medical reasons, an addition that gave her a piratical look in keeping with her liking to dress up, such as in military uniforms and tricorn hats.

Greta's known letters to Mercedes, while keeping emotions guarded, include many terms of endearment, such as "boy," "sweetie," and "honeychild." As their relationship went on, however, Mercedes may have been more infatuated with Greta than Greta was with her. Mercedes once wrote to Dietrich, "I do love [Greta] but I only love the person I have created and not the person who is real." In the end, no matter what Mercedes wanted, Greta just wanted to be alone.

James Baldwin

◇

Lucien Happersberger

Body and mind

1948–1987

> 66 Every lover [James] had after Lucien had to compete with the memory of him, the possibility of his return. 99

David Leeming, 2015

Black American writer and visionary James Baldwin had several relationships in his life, but there was one man he always longed for—bisexual Swiss painter Lucien Happersberger, whom he met in Paris in 1948 when he was 24 and Lucien 17. Their initial sexual attraction developed into a relationship of intense emotional power. When James fell into a bout of depression, Lucien invited him to his family's chalet in the Swiss Alps, where James finished his first novel, *Go Tell It On the Mountain* (1953), while Lucien cooked and painted.

James fell in love with Lucien—he dedicated his 1956 novel *Giovanni's Room* to him—and would continue to love him for the rest of his life, ever hopeful that they might one day live together. But within two years of their initial meeting, Lucien left James and married actress Diana Sands.

James continued to travel, and in the early 1960s went back to the US for a time to take part in the Civil Rights movement. After returning to Europe, he would write to his brother that Lucien was "the one real love story of my life." When James died of cancer at his French farmhouse in 1987, Lucien was sitting at his side.

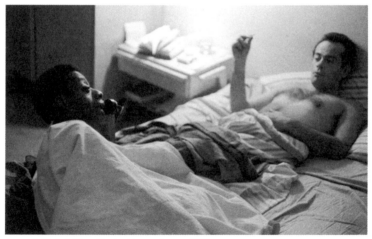

James Baldwin (left) and Lucien Happersberger, 1963

Grace Kelly

Prince Rainier III of Monaco

The best script ever

1955–1982

66 The idea of my life as a
fairy tale is itself a fairy tale. 99

Princess Grace, 1975

Prince Rainier and Grace Kelly in New York, in 1956

In May 1955, when a beautiful American movie star arrived for a photo session at the royal palace in Monaco, a spark ignited between her and the principality's ruler. Grace Kelly was 25 and had 11 films and an Academy Award to her credit. Rainier III was 31 and a bachelor.

The "wedding of the century," as it was dubbed by the press, captivated a worldwide television audience of 30 million, who gazed in wonder as Grace advanced up the aisle, six attendants holding her train, while the resplendently uniformed groom waited to make his entrance, as tradition in the principality dictated.

The royal couple smiled their way through the next quarter century. Behind the palace walls, though, all was not well. Never allowed to resume acting, Grace had only one role, that of Her Serene Highness the Princess of Monaco. Prince Rainier was rumored to be neglectful, and Grace often drunk and depressed. Whispers of infidelity circulated. Yet Prince Rainier was at her bedside when she died of injuries sustained in a car crash in September 1982. When Prince Rainier died 23 years later, he joined Princess Grace in the crypt of Monaco's cathedral, having never married again.

Forbidden love

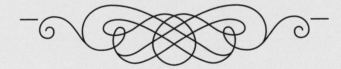

Abelard

Héloïse

From secret romance to tragedy

Early 12th century

The story of Héloïse and Abelard, two lovers in 12th-century France, contains many of the ingredients of a grand but doomed love affair—reckless pursuit and public scandal leading to painful separation and self-sacrifice. The lovers' lives and letters have inspired artists such as Edmund Leighton and Salvador Dalí, and writers ranging from Alexander Pope to Mark Twain.

The young Héloïse lived with her uncle Dr. Fulbert, a canon of the church of Notre-Dame in Paris. He doted on his niece, encouraged her brilliant mind, and educated her in the classics. Deciding that his protégé needed an exceptional tutor, Fulbert engaged the services of Peter Abelard, the founder of several schools of learning in Paris. He gave Abelard lodging in exchange for tutoring Héloïse.

Abelard was 37, while Héloïse was somewhere between 16 and her early twenties. Despite the age gap, this was a meeting of minds. As their lessons progressed, right under Fulbert's nose, their relationship became romantic. The two fell deeply in love and became intimate, even traveling to Fulbert's country home in Corbeil under the guise of study. Scandalous rumors circulated about the couple, but Fulbert did not become aware of their affair until he found them in bed together.

When Héloïse became pregnant, Abelard proposed marriage, but Héloïse argued against it, partly out of concern for Abelard's reputation as a teacher but also because she preferred "love to wedlock, freedom to a bond." She claimed she would rather be Abelard's "concubine or whore" than an empress to Augustus himself. Abelard hoped Héloïse would change her mind once the baby was born and arranged for her to give birth at his sister's home in Brittany, a plan that enraged Héloise's uncle, who feared for her reputation.

After the birth of their son Astrolabe, Abelard and Héloïse married in an early morning ceremony at Notre-Dame, with a few close friends and Fulbert in attendance. However, the family

> **❝ More were the kisses than the learned opinions. ❞**
>
> **Abelard**, *c.* 1132

> " Remember I still love you, and
> yet strive to avoid loving you. "

Héloïse, *c.* 1130–1140

disagreements continued. While Fulbert spread the news of the marriage, Héloïse took pains to deny it, still anxious to protect her independence. To escape her uncle's wrath, she fled to a convent at Argenteuil, near Paris, where Abelard visited her in secret.

Enraged by the deception, Fulbert sent men to ambush Abelard in the night and forcibly castrate him. This horrific assault immediately changed everything. Abelard became a monk, and Héloïse a nun. The orders taken by Héloïse and Abelard dissolved their marriage and the couple lost contact for many years.

In 1132, Abelard wrote a record of his struggles in his monastic life, entitled *Historia Calamitatum* (*A Story of Misfortunes*), with no mention of Héloïse. On learning of the document, Héloïse wrote a series of impassioned letters to Abelard, accusing him of neglecting her and bemoaning her life in the convent, but also full of longing and desire. While still loving, Abelard's letters were noticeably cooler, cautioning her to embrace monastic life and reconcile herself with her faith. Thanks to these letters, the enduring love between Héloïse and Abelard was immortalized.

Héloïse and Abelard spent the rest of their lives under monastic orders, becoming two of the foremost scholars of their day. Héloïse would eventually become the first abbess of the Abbaye du Paraclet, in Champagne, and make a name for herself through her writings. With nothing to do but dedicate herself to study, she produced works of staggering intellect, full of progressive views on marriage, menstruation, and women's roles.

The lovers were not reunited until after Abelard's death in 1142. According to his wishes, his body was sent to Héloïse's chapel at the Abbaye du Paraclet. Some legends say that when Héloïse herself died, 21 years later, she was buried beside him—and that his skeleton opened its arms to hold her again.

Abelard and his pupil Héloïse by Edmund Leighton, 1882

The Lovers of Teruel

Young love thwarted

c.1212–1217

The lovers of Teruel have been part of the Spanish cultural imagination since at least the 16th century. There are some variations to their story, which took place in the town of Teruel in eastern Spain in the 13th century. Essentially, Isabel de Segura and Diego Marcilla wanted to marry against her father's wishes. Arguing that Diego was too poor, her father gave him five years—some sources say seven—to leave Teruel and amass a fortune. If by the end of that time he failed to return a wealthy man, Isabel would marry his rival. Diego agreed to this challenge and left to become a mercenary soldier.

On the last day of the five years, Diego had still not come back, so Isabel was forced to marry the other man. One day later, Diego returned with his hard-earned riches. Tragically, he had not included the day of the arrangement when calculating five years. Diego asked Isabel to kiss him goodbye, but she refused out of respect for her new husband. In his grief, Diego fell down at Isabel's feet and died. At Diego's funeral, Isabel gave him the goodbye kiss, after which she, too, died of grief. According to legend, they were buried in the same grave.

Edward II

Piers Gaveston

Infatuated with the god Mars

1300–1312

It was love at first meeting when the young Prince Edward, son of Edward I of England, met Piers Gaveston, the son of a knight from Gascony. According to one contemporary observer, Edward immediately bound himself to the other man for eternity, "with a bond of indissoluble love." Piers was accomplished and a strong fighter, so the king brought him into the royal household to be Edward's companion. The king couldn't have imagined that Piers would prove the defining love of Edward's life.

The major obstacle to Edward and Piers's relationship was the English nobility. In 1307, the king banished Piers to appease the barons, who worried about Piers's influence on the young prince. When Edward was crowned Edward II later that year, he called Piers back to England and gave him titles and finery. Edward made Piers Earl of Cornwall, arranged an advantageous marriage for him, and spent most of his time with him, all but ignoring his wife and the barons. Piers was happy to flaunt his status, and attended Edward's coronation in purple robes (a color reserved for the monarch) trimmed with pearls; contemporary accounts describe him as dressed "more like the god Mars than a mere mortal."

Edward's patronage of Piers alienated his natural supporters. After two more unsuccessful attempts to exile him, Piers was captured and beheaded by the Earl of Warwick in 1312. Edward himself was later overthrown and imprisoned by his own wife. He died in 1327 while in Berkeley Castle, probably murdered.

Inês de Castro

Pedro I

Love, murder, and revenge

1339–1355

The story of how Pedro I, King of Portugal, came to be known as "Pedro the Cruel" is a tragic tale of doomed love. In 1339, before becoming king, Pedro had fallen in love with Inês de Castro, a lady-in-waiting of Constança Manuel, his new bride. The couple began an affair, often meeting in the gardens of what would later be known as the Quinta das Lágrimas (Estate of Tears) in the city of Coimbra.

When King Afonso IV heard about his son's secret relationship, he expelled Inês from court. However, when Constança died in 1345, Pedro was reunited with Inês. The couple lived together as though they were married, even raising children.

Afonso, who saw the relationship as immoral, was infuriated. When rumors circulated that the couple had married without his consent, Afonso plotted Inês's murder. In January 1355, while Pedro was away hunting, Inês was beheaded by Afonso's henchmen.

Inês's murder turned the father and son against each other, and civil war broke out in the kingdom. When Pedro ascended the throne in 1357, he avenged Inês's death, tracking down her murderers and allegedly ripping out their hearts. Pedro publicly declared that he and Inês had married before her death, which made her the country's legitimate queen. Legend has it that when Pedro moved her body from Coimbra to Alcobaça, near Lisbon, in 1360, he had it anointed. Afterward, Pedro laid Inês to rest in the royal pantheon of Alcobaça Monastery, where he would eventually join her in 1367. Their twin tombs can be seen today.

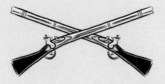

Ladislao Gutiérrez

◆

Camila O'Gorman

Passion, politics, and the Church

c.1846–1848

When newly ordained priest Ladislao Gutiérrez arrived in Buenos Aires to work in a local parish, he soon found himself falling in love with one of his parishioners—Camila O'Gorman, whose family were wealthy supporters of Juan Manuel de Rosas, the Governor of Buenos Aires. Despite Ladislao's pledge of celibacy, the couple began an affair, and in 1847 eloped, fleeing the city on horseback.

As news of the couple's disappearance spread through Buenos Aires, Rosas' political rivals blamed him for Camila's corruption. Mindful of moral disapproval, Rosas publicly shamed the pair—irrevocably damaging Camila's reputation. In June 1848, Ladislao and Camila, by then married and expecting their first child, were spotted in the city of Goya, where they had opened a school. After their arrest, Rosas refused to hold a trial and ordered their execution, despite a law preventing the execution of a pregnant woman. On August 18, 1848, the couple, along with their unborn child, were killed by firing squad, triggering worldwide condemnation of Rosas.

Alfred Douglas
—•—
Oscar Wilde

The aristocrat and the playwright

1891–1900

> " My dearest boy,
> This is to assure you
> of my immortal,
> my eternal love for you. "

Oscar Wilde, 1895

When Irish playwright Oscar Wilde first met Lord Alfred Douglas— known as "Bosie" since childhood—in 1892, Oscar was in his mid-thirties and married with two children. Alfred was a 21-year-old student at Oxford University. A fan of Wilde's work, Alfred was a budding writer himself, with poetry published in *The Chameleon*, a university journal.

Bosie fell in love with Oscar's wit, wealth, and fame, and Oscar with Bosie's golden beauty. The first poem Oscar wrote to Bosie, ends with the line "And I shall weep and worship as before"— presaging their many breakups and reunions in the years to come. The highs were magical, the arguments terrible, and the lows devastating.

The legal and social repercussions of their love, at a time when homosexuality was a criminal offense in Britain, would ultimately destroy Oscar's life, costing him his reputation, health, family, and privileged status in society. From 1895, Alfred's father, the Marquess of Queensberry, suspecting the nature of their relationship and blaming Oscar for his son's failure at university, began to harass the lovers and threatened to thrash them if he saw them out in public together. When Queensberry left Oscar a note at his club, accusing him of posing as a sodomite, Oscar, encouraged by Bosie, sued him for libel. The decision backfired. Instead of intimidating Queensberry, it hardened his determination to destroy Oscar. The case ended when Oscar, realizing he could not prove libel, as the charge was essentially true, withdrew. Based on testimony in the libel trial, Oscar was arrested for sodomy and indecency and jailed awaiting trial. Productions of his plays in London and New York closed and his books were withdrawn from sale, leaving him without an income.

The prosecuting counsel found young men to testify that they had received money for engaging in sexual acts with Oscar, which were illegal under the Criminal Law Amendment Act of 1885. When the jury couldn't come to a verdict, there was a retrial. Oscar was found guilty and sentenced to two years' hard labor. Prison conditions were harsh; Oscar was tied to a treadmill for six hours a day and had to sleep on a wooden plank.

Oscar was also destroyed financially. His home, personal library, art collection, and other belongings were sold to pay the court costs. His wife Constance moved to Switzerland with their two sons and changed their last name to Holland to avoid the notoriety, but she wrote to Oscar and continued to send him money. Alfred wrote letters to newspapers defending Oscar and petitioned Queen Victoria for Oscar's release, but without success.

While in Reading Jail, Oscar wrote *De Profundis*, Latin for "from the depths," in essence a long love letter to Bosie. The work was a mix of love and bitterness, containing reflections on his love for Bosie, frustrations with him and his father, and meditations on suffering, art, and forgiveness. Extracts from *De Profundis* were published in 1905 and 1908, but a complete version faithful to the original manuscript would not appear until 1962.

Oscar left prison in May 1897, and three months later, he and Alfred reunited in France and then moved to Italy, living for a few months in Villa Giudice in Naples. In a letter to a friend, Oscar wrote, "The mere fact that he wrecked my life makes me love him." The relationship ended when Alfred's mother and Wilde's wife cut off their funds. Oscar moved to Paris, but wrote only one more work, *The Ballad of Reading Gaol* (1898), a plea for prison reform. His health had deteriorated in prison, and he died of meningitis in November 1900.

Oscar Wilde is now celebrated as a great writer and a courageous early champion of sexual freedom. Like so many artists and visionaries who led bold lives ahead of their times, Oscar would ultimately gain global adulation only after his death.

Against the law

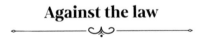

Homosexuality was outlawed in England during the reign of Henry VIII. The 1553 Buggery Act made sodomy—until then, considered immoral rather than criminal—punishable by death, and it remained a capital offense until 1861. In 1885, 10 years before Oscar Wilde stood trial, all "acts of gross indecency" between men were criminalized (lesbians were excluded, as they were considered rare, if not unimaginable), widening the range of illegal activities. This law remained in place in Britain until 1967, when the Sexual Offences Act decriminalized homosexual acts between adults over 21 in private.

" I am the love that dare not speak its name. "

Alfred Douglas, 1892

Oscar Wilde (standing) and "Bosie" in 1893

ALFRED DOUGLAS & OSCAR WILDE

Lili Elbe
•
Gerda Wegener

A tale of two women
1904–1930

Lili Elbe and Gerda Wegener (née Gottlieb) were married for 25 years. At first, their relationship was happy. Lili, who had been assigned male at birth, had met Gerda at the Royal Danish Academy of Fine Arts in Copenhagen. They had fallen in love, and married in 1904, when Lili was 21 and Gerda 19.

Lili was a successful landscape artist, who won Denmark's prestigious Neuhausen Prize in 1907. Gerda, on the other hand, painted lesbian erotica and fashionable women, and it was her work that led to an epiphany in Lili. One day, in need of a model, Gerda asked her husband to pose for her in women's clothes. After these sessions, Lili realized she was a woman, and the couple began to go out as two women, Lili pretending to be Gerda's cousin. The pair moved to Paris in 1912, and Gerda's work became popular, winning accolades at the 1925 World's Fair. While Gerda thrived, however, Lili suffered; by 1930, she was increasingly uncomfortable with her body and made the choice to medically transition rather than to die by suicide. As marriage between two women was illegal, it was annulled by the Danish king.

Lili then underwent five surgeries, and began to cut ties with her old life, taking Elbe as a last name. Tragically, she did not survive the fifth round of surgery. In 1931, without telling Gerda, she underwent a procedure to implant ovaries and a uterus, and died of complications soon after. Gerda's second marriage and later career were largely unsuccessful; she died, poor and obscure, in 1940.

Gerda's *Air de Capri* of 1923 depicts Gerda (left) and Lili while they were married.

" My husband, my friend,
my comrade—has now become
a woman, a complete woman. "

Gerda Wegener, *c* 1930

Edward VIII

◆

Wallis Simpson

The ruler ruled by his heart

1931–1972

In January 1931, Edward, the playboy Prince of Wales and future heir to the British throne, was introduced to Mrs. Wallis Simpson at an English country house party. Wallis, who had divorced her first husband and was still married to her second, was sophisticated and witty. Her charm concealed a dark side—rumors of infidelity, ruthless social climbing, and closet fascism—but that did not bother Edward, who had fascist sympathies, too. If Edward did not fall in love with Wallis at first sight, he did soon afterward—to the despair of his father, King George V.

George V died in January 1936 and the turbulent 326-day reign of King Edward VIII began, dominated by the new king's insistence on marrying Wallis. The Church of England, of which Edward was titular head, frowned upon any marriage with a divorced person whose former spouses were still living, an objection reinforced by the royal family and the government. Edward refused to give up Wallis, and on December 10, 1936, signed the Instrument of Abdication, surrendering the throne to his younger brother, George VI. The following day, Edward announced his abdication in a radio broadcast to the world.

Edward and Wallis were married within six months. Now styled the Duke and Duchess of Windsor, the couple spent decades leading an indolent, dissolute life wandering the globe as pampered expatriates. When the Duke died in Paris in 1972, at the age of 77, his body was returned to Britain and buried in the Royal Burial Ground outside Windsor Castle; when Wallis died 14 years later, she was buried by his side.

> " I have found it impossible to carry the heavy burden of responsibility ... without the help and support of the woman I love. "

Edward VIII, 1936

The Duke and Duchess in 1953

Seretse Khama
Ruth Williams Khama

Love across a racial divide

1948–1980

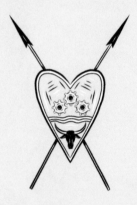

66 The smile on her face told me what
I wanted to know. She did love me,
and I knew for certain that this was
the woman I wanted for my wife. 99

Seretse Khama, 1951

Ruth and Seretse overlooking Bechuanaland in 1950

The wedding of African law student Seretse Khama and English insurance underwriter's clerk Ruth Williams in September 1948 was simplicity itself—held at a register office in London. At the time, though, it was front page news, for the groom was *kgosi* (king) of the Bamangwato people of the British protectorate of Bechuanaland (now Botswana). In Bechuanaland, Seretse's uncle tried to stop the marriage; in neighboring South Africa, the apartheid government, intent on imposing racial segregation, put pressure on Britain to do the same. In 1949, Seretse took his now pregnant wife home, where the couple won the approval of the council of elders. The colonial authorities, however, remained opposed, and the pair returned to England with their new daughter. Only in 1956, after a worldwide outcry, did London relent— they could live in Bechuanaland if Seretse renounced the kingship.

Returning to Bechuanaland as a private citizen, Seretse became prime minister in 1965, and president of a newly independent Botswana the following year. Seretse died in office in 1980; Ruth stayed in her adopted homeland, where she died in 2002.

Frank Merlo

·

Tennessee Williams

Acts of love

1948–1963

The American playwright Tennessee Williams spent 14 years with the love of his life, Frank Merlo, during which he enjoyed the most productive and creative phase of his career. Tennessee met Frank, the New Jersey–born son of Italian immigrants, in a bar in Provincetown, Massachusetts, in the summer of 1947, and the pair had a passionate one-night stand on the beach. A year later, the men met again by chance in a New York deli. Sparks flew, and they embarked upon a romantic relationship.

Frank proved a stabilizing influence in Tennessee's chaotic life, helping him kick drugs in order to write some of his most successful works: Tennessee had six plays shown on Broadway in the 1950s, and won two Pulitzer Prizes. One of his most famous plays, *The Rose Tattoo*, was inspired by Frank and their summers together in Italy with Frank's extended family. Unusually for Tennessee's work, the play has a happy ending, and is dedicated to their love and travels together: "To Frankie in Return For Sicily."

Their happiness, however, did not last. They broke up twice—once in 1961, and finally in 1963. According to Tennessee, the second breakup came after a blazing argument in which Frank threw a whole leg of lamb at his lover. Had Frank not been diagnosed with lung cancer in 1963, the two might not have reconnected. Frank died later that year, but until the end of his life, Tennessee never found another man he would love as much.

Tennessee Williams (left) and Frank Merlo

66 He was so close to life.
He tied me down to earth. 99

Tennessee Williams, 1981

Mildred Loving
—◆———◆—
Richard Loving

Love triumphs
1958–1975

In the small hours of July 14, 1958, police burst into the bedroom of newlyweds Richard and Mildred Loving and demanded to know why they were in bed together. When the couple pointed to their marriage license on the wall, the sheriff hauled them off to jail. Their crime was breaking a Virginia law that prohibited interracial marriage: Richard was white and Mildred was mixed race. The couple had married in Washington, D. C., but the Virginia statute extended to interracial marriages performed outside the state.

Convicted and sentenced to one year in prison, the Lovings were offered a suspended sentence if they left Virginia for 25 years. They moved to Washington, D.C., but longed to return to the tiny town of Central Point, where they had grown up in a racially mixed close-knit community of families and friends who enjoyed music and drag-racing. By law, Mildred and Richard had attended segregated schools, but Richard's best friends were Black or mixed race and he had met Mildred while visiting her older brothers to listen to guitar and fiddle music. Mildred had thought him "arrogant" at first but eventually became fond of the family friend, and the pair fell in love. They married when she became pregnant at the age of 18.

In 1964, Mildred, feeling exiled from loved ones, wrote to Attorney General Robert Kennedy, who referred her to the American Civil Liberties Union (ACLU). Eventually, the

Mildred and Richard after the 1967 Supreme Court ruling legitimizing their marriage

US Supreme Court ruled in 1967 that state bans on interracial marriage were unconstitutional. The Lovings moved back to Central Point, where Richard, a bricklayer, built his family a home.

Mildred and Richard became the symbol of the landmark decision that gave Americans the freedom to marry regardless of race. Richard perished in a car accident in 1975. When Mildred died in 2008, she was buried beside him in the cemetery down the road from their house.

> " Not a day goes by that I don't
> think of Richard and our love
> and the right ... to marry the person
> precious to me. "

Mildred Loving, 2007

Tragic love

Mark Antony

◆

Cleopatra

Together forever

c. 41–30 BCE

History knows Cleopatra as the wily Egyptian queen who seduced two Roman rulers, first Julius Caesar and then Mark Antony. But her story was written by victorious Romans as part of a propaganda war by Octavian, the Roman ruler who caused her downfall. The truth of the last pharaoh to rule Egypt and her lovers is more complex.

Historians agree that Cleopatra was rich, charming, witty, intelligent, and fluent in many languages. In 51 BCE, her father died and her 10-year-old brother succeeded him, ruling as Ptolemy XIII. According to Egyptian tradition, the siblings married but they soon clashed over control of the kingdom, and Cleopatra was exiled. Their power struggle became embroiled in the dispute between the Roman general Pompey and Julius Caesar. During that conflict, Ptolemy drowned and Pompey was assassinated.

When Julius Caesar arrived in Egypt in 48 BCE, the 21-year-old queen began an affair with him to win his help in securing the throne. He made her queen of Egypt and she gave him a son, Caesarion.

When Caesar returned to Rome, Cleopatra followed, and the Roman emperor and the Egyptian queen continued their affair under his wife's nose. After the assassination of Caesar in 44 BCE, Cleopatra returned to Egypt.

In 41 BCE, Cleopatra became embroiled in another Roman power struggle, this time between Caesar's adopted son Octavian and his most trusted general, Mark Antony, two of the three men ruling Rome. It was one she would not survive.

Mark Antony, in charge of Rome's Eastern Empire, ordered Cleopatra to meet with him in Southern Turkey. Never the supplicant, she arrived in style, sailing up the Cydnus River dressed as Isis, the Egyptian goddess of love. Her barge was gold with purple sails, and girls dressed as nymphs plied silver oars. Roman historian Plutarch reports that, at 28, Cleopatra was "in the time of life when women's beauty is most splendid and their intellects are in full maturity." Antony, then 42, was first charmed and then completely smitten.

The handsome general and the glamorous queen fell madly in love. She took him back to Alexandria, where they spent the winter enjoying themselves, but their romantic idyll came to an end when Antony returned to Rome and entered into a political marriage with Octavian's sister, Octavia. Back in Egypt, Cleopatra gave birth to twins, Alexander Helios and Cleopatra Selene. The boy was named for the god of the sun, and the girl for the goddess of the moon.

When Antony and Cleopatra were reunited in Syria three years later, their passion rekindled. Antony gave Cleopatra gifts of land, making her ruler of most of the eastern Mediterranean. Cleopatra and

> " Age cannot wither her,
> nor custom stale
> Her infinite variety; other women cloy
> The appetites they feed, but she
> makes hungry where most she satisfies. "

William Shakespeare, *Antony and Cleopatra*, 1606

her retinue traveled with Antony as he and his soldiers pursued their goal of conquering the world for Rome. When he defeated Armenia, the sight of its king and queen being paraded through the streets of Alexandria in chains was one that Cleopatra would not forget.

Flushed with success, Antony and Cleopatra flaunted their power by staging a coronation ceremony. Mark Antony sat on one golden throne and Cleopatra, whom he called the "New Isis," sat on another. Cleopatra's four children—her son by Caesar, the twins, and a little boy born after their reunion—sat on child-size silver thrones at their feet. Antony gave them all lands, setting them up as a new dynasty in the East.

Word of this extravagant event infuriated Octavian and the citizens of Rome. Antony was taking possession of lands he had conquered for Rome, and which therefore belonged to Rome. Octavian headed to Egypt at the head of a Roman army that Antony and Cleopatra could not match. Defeated, they fled to Alexandria, where the final act played out. Told that Cleopatra had died by suicide, Antony stabbed himself, but before he breathed his last, Cleopatra appeared and he died in her arms. For the sake of her children, Cleopatra tried to negotiate with Octavian but to no avail. Kept a prisoner, her lover dead, and remembering the Roman custom of parading deposed leaders in front of jeering crowds, Cleopatra ended her life. Some say she took poison; others that she put an asp to her breast. In death, she and Antony were reunited and, according to her last wishes, were buried side by side.

Queen of Hollywood

Elizabeth Taylor played Cleopatra in the 1963 film version of Shakespeare's play and lost her heart to her Antony, Richard Burton. Their torrid, often drunken, affair started with an on-screen kiss that continued long after the director yelled "Cut!" They married, divorced, married again, and divorced for good in 1976. Taylor married eight times, and claimed the love of her life was not Burton but Michael Todd, her second husband, who died in a plane crash in 1958.

" The moment he saw her,
Antony lost his head to her
like a young man. "

Appian, 2nd century CE

Antinous

–––◆–––

Hadrian

Lovers in arms

123–130 CE

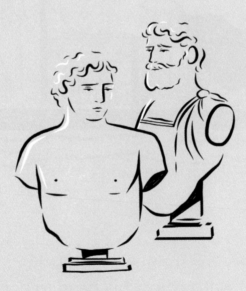

When Roman Emperor Hadrian lost his lover Antinous in an accident in 130 CE, he made his people worship this ordinary man from Bithynia as a god. Hadrian went on a tour of the empire three years after becoming emperor. One of the stops was Claudiopolis (now in Turkey), where Hadrian and Antinous met for the first time in 123 CE. Antinous, who was then only 12 (Hadrian was around 47), went to Rome soon after.

Hadrian was married, but had no interest in women. Instead, he had several male favorites. By the time Antinous was 17, the young man had become Hadrian's most beloved companion. Taking a male lover was common practice for a Roman emperor. Relationships between older men and beardless youths—with a disparity in age, power, and status—were common in Roman society, but were usually purely physical. In the case of Hadrian and Antinous, however, the relationship was one of mutual adoration. When Antinous grew into a strong man—even saving Hadrian's life while on a lion hunt in Libya—the relationship continued.

" The deified Ganymede of Hadrian. "

Aurelius Prudentius Clemens, 348–c.413

Antinous soon began to accompany Hadrian on his travels, but ru mors about the nature of their relationship began to circulate. The gossip came to a head in Egypt, where the emperor and his retinue paraded down the Nile in a stately procession. According to Hadrian, a terrible accident occurred, and his beloved fell into the Nile and drowned. Hadrian was consumed by grief at the loss of Antinous. He honored his memory by building an entire city on the banks of the Nile in his lover's name. Antinous was made a demigod in the city, and the cult of Antinous spread to at least 80 cities in the empire, with many statues made in his likeness. Hadrian himself died in 138 CE. The cult of Antinous outlived them both, just as Hadrian had wanted. His image remains a symbol of classical male beauty.

Yang Guifei

◊

Xuanzong

A match made in imperial China

8th century CE

The Tang dynasty presided over a golden age in Chinese history, but one emperor's love for his concubine would bring it to its knees. Emperor Xuanzong first met the young Yang Guifei when she was presented as a concubine for his son, the Prince of Shou. At the time, the emperor was married to his first wife, Wu Huifei, but after her death in 737 CE, he was free to pursue Yang. Yang was the most beautiful woman in China, and women at court tried to emulate her plump figure.

According to legends, one day Xuanzong permitted Yang to bathe at the Huaqing hot springs. This was a high honor, as the springs were for the emperor's family and high-ranking officials only. The Tang poets describe how the emperor watched Yang emerge from the water and immediately fell in love with her. Xuanzong arranged for Yang to become a Daoist nun so that her marriage would be voided, and in 745 CE, she was made "Guifei," his imperial consort.

Xuanzong began to neglect his responsibilities in favor of a decadent life with Yang, buying her fresh lychees from the south, which arrived by courier, and spending late nights dancing and drinking fine wines from Sichuan with her. He also allowed Yang to influence his government, and agreed to support both her cousin, Yang Guozhong, who rose rapidly through the court, and her protégé, an ambitious half-Turkish army officer named An Lushan.

In 755 CE, Yang Guifei's influence proved fatal. An Lushan turned against Yang Guozhong and the emperor in a military rebellion that threatened the whole empire. The emperor was forced to flee to Sichuan, but Yang did not survive the journey. The imperial guard mutinied en route, blaming her for all the empire's troubles, and forced the emperor to order his lover's execution. Yang was either strangled by a court eunuch or ordered to die by suicide.

> " She was his
> springtime mistress,
> and his midnight tyrant—
> two birds on the same wing. "
>
> **Bai Juyi**, C.809 CE

Alexander Hamilton

Eliza Hamilton

The founding father and the socialite

1780–1804

A lexander and Eliza Hamilton met in the maelstrom of America's war for independence and married after a whirlwind courtship. On the face of it, the marriage was unequal. Elizabeth "Eliza" Schuyler came from a prominent New York family; Alexander Hamilton was the illegitimate son of a Scottish trader in the West Indies, and his New York education had been provided by charity. However, Alexander had risen through the ranks of the Continental Army and become the most trusted aide of General George Washington.

Alexander and Eliza probably met for the first time at her family's home in Albany, where Alexander briefly stayed on his travels through New York in 1778. Little is known about how much they

" Love me I conjure you. "

Alexander Hamilton, 1780

talked together during his stay. Their more important meeting happened in 1780, when Eliza's aunt threw a winter ball at her home near Morristown, New Jersey, and invited Washington's staff as her esteemed guests. It was here that the dashing young officer and the charming young socialite set their sights on one another.

Before meeting Eliza in 1780, Alexander had gained a reputation as a ladies' man, with his good looks and quick wit. Despite his relative poverty and lack of a good family name, he was popular. Eliza's father's money and name were no doubt attractive to him, but she was also a captivating woman. Meeting her again at the ball, Alexander monopolized Eliza, enlisting her sister Peggy to distract any rivals.

From that night on, Alexander and Eliza began an intense correspondence, and it was not long before he was writing to Philip Schuyler to ask for his daughter's hand in marriage. The match won her father's approval and the two married at the Schuyler family home in December 1780.

When the war ended, Alexander continued to prosper under Washington's patronage. He earned a law degree, joined the Continental Congress, and went on to become the first Secretary of the Treasury of the United States in 1789. Eliza, meanwhile, supported him, not just emotionally and financially, but by offering advice and acting as a sounding board for his ideas. Some of Alexander's early notes on the US financial system are in Eliza's handwriting.

Eliza and Alexander were married for 24 years, during which they had eight children. The pair struggled financially, refusing assistance from Eliza's family, but otherwise seemed to live happily until 1797, when their marriage hit a stumbling block. That year, Alexander published the "Reynolds Pamphlet," in which he admitted to a year-long affair with a woman named Maria Reynolds, who had sought his help in New York while Eliza and the children were at home in Albany. Alexander published the paper because he was being blackmailed by Maria's husband, who threatened to expose the affair.

Eliza and Alexander Hamilton

" Neither time distance nor any other circumstance can abate that pure that holy that ardent flame which burns in my bosom for the best and sweetest of her sex. "

Alexander Hamilton, 1781

The pamphlet damaged Alexander's marriage and his reputation. Eliza, who was pregnant with their sixth child, was heartbroken, and moved to her parents' house to escape the scandal.

Somehow Eliza found it in her heart to forgive Alexander, but the affair—and the subsequent death of their eldest son (see below)—was not the end of the family's troubles. In 1804, Alexander was challenged to a duel by Aaron Burr, a long-time acquaintance who accused him of ruining his career. Alexander had championed Burr's rival candidate—the husband of his sister-in-law Peggy—in the New York election for governor. The pair met at the New Jersey dueling grounds. While Alexander intended to aim his pistol away from Burr, Burr noted that his opponent was wearing glasses, and believed he would shoot to kill. When the call came to shoot, Burr fatally wounded Alexander, who died with Eliza at his side.

The loss of Alexander left Eliza alone with seven children and a pile of debts. She scraped together funds for both her family and various charitable causes, showing a head for finances and a passion for restoring her husband's name. Just as his writings had shaped the new nation, her work influenced the founding fathers' legacy. She sent questionnaires to Alexander's military compatriots, which formed the basis of historical knowledge about the war, and lobbied for funds for monuments to its heroes. Most importantly, she secured Alexander's place in the American story, getting his many writings edited and published. Eliza's death in 1854, at the age of 97, ended a life characterized by great strength and unwavering devotion.

The death of their eldest son

In 1801, Alexander and Eliza's eldest son, Philip, was killed in a duel trying to defend his father's name. Philip was his father's son in many ways—handsome and clever, with a bright future ahead of him. But one night, at the theater, he encountered George Eacker, who had attacked his father in a speech. Philip stormed Eacker's box, prompting Eacker to challenge him to a duel. Three days later, Philip carried the same pistols his father would later use to the dueling grounds. Alexander advised Philip to either not fire or fire into the air, but Eacker had no such qualms. He shot and killed Alexander and Eliza's beloved son.

Mary Shelley

·

Percy Bysshe Shelley

Her heart's desire

1814–1822

Early one morning in July 1814, 17-year-old Mary Wollstonecraft Godwin tiptoed out her father's house in London to elope with 22-year-old poet Percy Bysshe Shelley. The daughter of Mary Wollstonecraft, the mother of feminism, and anarchist William Godwin, Mary was a born rebel; Shelley, the grandson of a wealthy baronet and already married with a child, embraced radical ideals.

Eight years of struggle and high drama followed, much of it in continental Europe. Shelley's free love convictions led to numerous liaisons, while Mary endured emotional deprivation and watched three of their four children die in infancy. Grinding poverty in a gloomy château rented by their friend Lord Byron on the shores of Lake Geneva was punctuated by periods of creative frenzy. In 1822, Shelley drowned in a sailing accident off Italy, at the age of 29. His body was cremated on the beach, but his heart was retained and eventually given to Mary.

Out of the cauldron of the couple's suffering emerged some of the finest lyric poetry in the English language, as well as Mary's Gothic novel *Frankenstein*. Mary lived mostly in England for the remaining 29 years of her life, writing historical novels and lifting her lost Percy from relative obscurity up to everlasting fame by editing and publishing his works. When she died at the age of 53 in 1851, her surviving son, who inherited the Shelley family baronetcy, found the remains of Shelley's heart among her prized possessions, wrapped carefully in silk.

Czar Nicholas

◇

Czarina Alexandra

Love imperial

1894–1918

The Russian love story that ended in front of a Bolshevik firing squad in 1918 began 34 years earlier in St. Petersburg's Winter Palace. There, at the wedding of his uncle, Grand Duke Sergei, to a German princess, the teenage Nicholas Romanov, heir apparent to the Russian throne, met the bride's sister, Alix. A second visit to Russia by Alix in 1890 cemented the mutual attraction.

Initially, Nicholas's father, Czar Alexander III, opposed the match, but by 1894, with his health deteriorating, he relented. By the year's end, Alexander III had died and Alix had married Czar Nicholas II.

Nicholas's weak government, combined with a terrible famine and high Russian casualties in World War I, helped topple the czarist regime, and in March 1917, Nicholas abdicated. A provisional government sent the imperial family to Tobolsk in Siberia and then to the Urals for their safety, but on July 17, 1918, the new revolutionary Bolshevik government executed the couple, their children, and their loyal servants in the basement of a house in Yekaterinburg.

Richard Feynman

·———·

Arline Greenbaum

Getting metaphysical

1941–1945

" I am alone without you and you were the 'idea-woman' and general instigator of our wild adventures. **"**

Richard Feynman, 1946

Richard and Arline

Richard Feynman was a brilliant young physicist from Queens, New York, at the start of his career. Arline Greenbaum, his fiancée, had been diagnosed with incurable tuberculosis. It was June 1942, six months after the US entry into World War II, and Richard had been working on a secret project (known as the Manhattan Project) to develop the atomic bomb. He married his adored "Putzie" on June 29.

When the project was relocated to Los Alamos, New Mexico, Arline stayed in a sanatorium where he could visit her once a week. He did this for two years, also writing daily letters. The letters breathe their love, along with a hope against hope that she would get better. She did not. In June 1945, she died.

Feynman's career culminated in a Nobel Prize in 1965. A second marriage ended in divorce, but he found happiness with his third wife, and had two children. After his death, his daughter found a letter to "D'Arline" written in October 1946, over a year after her death. He tells her how much he misses her, and adds in a postscript, "Please excuse my not mailing this—but I don't know your new address."

Manolete

—◊—

Lupe Sino

The matador and the actress

1943–1947

Born in 1917 to a family of bullfighters in Córdoba, Spain, Manolete was destined to be in the ring. He first performed at age 17 and quickly became recognized as one of Spain's greatest bullfighters. Dedicated to his work, the young matador appeared to have no interest in love.

One evening in 1943, Manolete was in the Chicote bar in Madrid when an acquaintance walked in with an attractive young woman—an actress known as Lupe Sino. Immediately captivated by the stranger's beauty, Manolete urged his friend to introduce him to her. The pair clicked, and a few dates turned into true love.

The match was immediately met with hostility, especially from Manolete's controlling mother. The matador's entourage saw the modern young woman as a threat, only interested in his money and fame, and called her "the snake." Despite their disapproval, the relationship continued. Over the next few years, he began to travel with Lupe and spent less time in the ring. The pair set a date for their wedding—October 18, 1947—and Manolete planned to retire.

Manolete's career did not end in the series of final triumphs he intended. On August 28, 1947, a bull fatally gored him in the small bullring at Linares. His entourage refused to let Lupe see the dying Manolete, perhaps fearing he would marry her in his final moments, leaving her his fortune. Manolete died in hospital in the early hours of the following morning, with Lupe outside his room, still waiting to be let in.

> 66 I know that, had they let me be by his side that night in Linares, he would have married me. 99

Lupe Sino

Marcel Cerdan

Edith Piaf

The boxer and the little sparrow

1947–1949

> " I wish that night could have gone on singing, spinning, laughing forever. "

Edith Piaf

The little black dress was Edith Piaf's trademark look and reflected some deep sadness. The life of the "little sparrow" of French song had been hard. She was brought up by her grandmother in a brothel in Pigalle, a red-light district of Paris, and sang her songs of love and loss, tragedy and pain, from the heart, arms outstretched in supplication.

In 1947, Edith found what she had been looking for all her life: love. He was the French-Algerian boxer Marcel Cerdan, known as the Casablanca Clouter, who had fought his way up through the ranks in the boxing rings of North Africa. When they met, they were both at the top of their careers: he, soon to win the World Middleweight Championship, and she, a famous *chanteuse*. They had come a long way from the mean streets of their youth to find happiness in one another (despite the fact that he was already married).

Their love was shattered on October 27, 1949, when Marcel's flight to New York crashed, leaving no survivors. At his state funeral in Casablanca, thousands lined the streets. Edith Piaf lived on, wearing her usual black, and marrying twice more. But she was often lost to alcohol and painkillers, and in 1963 joined the love of her life in death.

Edith Piaf and Marcel Cerdan at a nightclub in 1948

Martin Luther King, Jr.

◆———————◆

Coretta Scott King

Two souls with one goal

1952–1968

❝ It was synergy. It was symphony.
Our destinies fused. **❞**

Coretta Scott King

Coretta and Martin in the late 1950s

In January 1952, Coretta Scott, a student at the New England Conservatory of Music in Boston, Massachusetts, was set up on a blind date with a PhD student in theology at Boston University. His name was Martin Luther King, Jr.

In some ways, the couple were very different. Where he was outgoing, she was introverted. The son of an Atlanta minister, Martin was also more financially secure than Coretta, who subsidized her studies by working as a maid. Yet the two fell in love and married in June 1953, moving to Montgomery, Alabama, in 1954.

The pair shared a commitment to civil rights, and Coretta sacrificed her dream of becoming a singer to support his activism. After an assassin murdered her husband in 1968, leaving her a single mother to four young children, she established the Martin Luther King, Jr., Memorial Center in Atlanta. Today, a mural honoring the couple's love stands at the former location of the Twelfth Baptist Church in the city where they first met. It's titled *Roxbury Love Story*.

Joy Davidman

◇

C. S. Lewis

Surprised by love

1956–1960

When lively, forthright New Yorker Joy Davidman first met English don C. S. ("Jack") Lewis in Oxford in 1952, the bond they formed was immediate and strong—but, on Jack's side at least, not even remotely romantic. Joy, who had been corresponding with Jack for two years, was a poet and novelist, mother of two young sons, and married to William Gresham, a fellow radical New York writer. Alongside his academic career, bachelor Jack was a committed Christian, who had found fame with books of popular theology and, more recently, his Narnia children's stories. Though from a Jewish family, Joy was a convert to Christianity, and had been influenced by Jack's theological books.

> " She was my daughter and my
> mother, my pupil and my teacher,
> my subject and my sovereign. "

C. S. Lewis, 1961

Back in New York, Joy had to accept the end of her troubled marriage to the alcoholic Gresham when he asked her for a divorce. She returned to England, where she rented a house near Jack's in Oxford. In 1956, as an act of convenience to permit her to stay in the UK, the pair married quietly in a civil ceremony but continued to live separately.

The next year, Joy tripped and broke her leg. In the hospital, doctors discovered she had incurable bone cancer. Only then did a distraught Jack realize the depth and passion of his feelings for her. Despite difficulties because she was a divorcee, he cajoled an Anglican priest friend into giving them a religious wedding at her hospital bedside.

In the end, Joy responded to radiation treatment, and three years of ecstatic happiness followed. A checkup in late 1959 revealed that the cancer had returned, and Joy died on July 13, 1960. Jack's moving account of his near despair at her loss, *A Grief Observed*, was published under a pseudonym the following year.

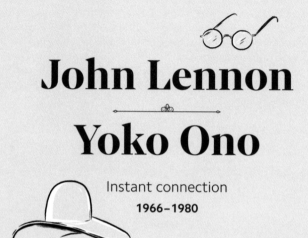

John Lennon

Yoko Ono

Instant connection
1966–1980

" We dig being together all the
time, and both of us could
survive apart, but what for. "

John Lennon, 1971

Beatle John Lennon and avant-garde artist Yoko Ono were on the same wavelength from the moment they met—at a preview of Yoko's exhibition *Unfinished Paintings and Objects* in London in 1966. On seeing the object *Hammer and Nails*—an empty board, a hammer attached to the board by a chain, and a pile of nails—John asked Yoko if he could hammer a nail into the board. She said no at first, but then said it would cost him five shillings. In the spirit of the piece, he said he would bang in an imaginary nail for an imaginary five shillings. He and Yoko connected.

Yoko and John's partnership was both personal and artistic. They recorded their first musical collaboration, *Unfinished Music No. 1: Two Virgins*, in an overnight session at his home in Surrey in May 1968. The album included a variety of improvised vocalizations, bird song, distorted instruments, and slowed-down tape effects. They chose photographs of themselves naked for the album cover, saying they wanted to show off their love for each other.

At the time, Yoko and John were married to other people—Yoko to American filmmaker Anthony Cox and John to Cynthia Lennon, his art school sweetheart from Liverpool—and each had a young child. Determined to be together, John and Yoko divorced their spouses and married in Gibraltar in March 1969. For their honeymoon, they held a seven day Bed-In for Peace at the Amsterdam Hilton to protest against the Vietnam War. A second Bed-In followed in Montreal, where they cowrote and recorded the anthem "Give Peace A Chance." (John later regretted giving Paul McCartney rather than Yoko joint credit for the song.) In other happenings, the couple gave interviews from inside a large white bag, commenting that their "bagism" was a great way to highlight their message. They also ran a billboard campaign stating "War Is Over! If You Want It."

John had become increasingly dissatisfied with the stifling reality of life as a Beatle, and Yoko gave him the renewed energy and optimism he craved. On August 20, 1969, she sat close to him through what would be the last recording session for the Beatles. Fittingly, one of the songs was "I Want You (She's So Heavy)," John's raw outpouring of love for Yoko. When the Beatles went their separate ways a month later, Yoko faced vitriol and ridicule from both the fans and the popular press, who blamed her for breaking up the group.

In 1971, John and Yoko left for New York, where they flirted with radical left politics before returning to peaceful activism. But the couple were under pressure. A threat of deportation from the US hung over John, because of a drug conviction in the UK, and Yoko was tired of being Mrs. Lennon. She worried that she was becoming invisible and her work was suffering.

Needing space from John in the summer of 1973, Yoko sent John to Los Angeles, where he started (with Yoko's blessing) a relationship with one of their personal assistants, May Pang. Away from Yoko, John drank heavily and partied hard, but he continued to make music and kept in close touch with Yoko. After 18 months of what John described as his "lost weekend," Yoko was ready to have him back. Later, he said their separation had been a failure.

Following two miscarriages, Yoko gave birth to their son Sean on October 9, 1975, John's own birthday. John stopped drinking, took an extended break from music, and became a house-husband while Yoko looked after their business affairs.

In August 1980, John and Yoko started work on their final album together, *Double Fantasy*. Subtitled "A Heart Play," it was conceived as a musical dialogue between two characters exploring their love for each other. At Yoko's insistence, the tracks alternated, so that hers could not be easily ignored in favor of John's. His comeback had been eagerly awaited but many critics found his new songs middle of the road while describing Yoko's as innovative and

Imagine

John Lennon's iconic song "Imagine" was inspired by poems in Yoko Ono's book *Grapefruit*, a collection of instructions for her conceptual art. On what would have been John's 45th birthday, Yoko dedicated Strawberry Fields peace garden in Central Park, New York City, to his memory. Its centerpiece is a black and white mosaic bearing the word "Imagine." Twelve years later, Yoko unveiled her Imagine Peace Tower near Reykjavik, Iceland, a tower of light projected into the sky from a wishing well inscribed with the words IMAGINE PEACE in 24 languages. The tower is lit up on John's birthday every year.

John and Yoko at their first Bed-In for Peace, 1969

> **" At least I had that,
> one guy understood me. "**

Yoko Ono, 2002

modern. Rather than being dismayed by his own poor reviews, John was excited about a dance track Yoko was recording—"Walking On Thin Ice"—thinking she could capitalize on her recent success by quickly releasing the track as a single. On December 8, 1980, John and Yoko spent the day in the studio putting the final touches on the song. That evening, as they arrived home at the Dakota apartment building, near Central Park, a fan approached John and shot and killed him in front of the love of his life. The whole world went into shock.

Miles Davis

◇

Cicely Tyson

Bolt from the blue

1965–1989

" Cicely is that type of woman who just gets into you, gets inside your blood and your head. **"**

Miles Davis, 1990

Miles and Cicely, 1983

Long before actress Cicely Tyson met Miles Davis in 1965, she was a big fan. The famous jazz trumpeter had spoken to her through his music, especially the innovative 1959 album *Kind of Blue*. Living in the same neighborhood, they ran into each other in Riverside Park, a scenic waterfront in Manhattan. The couple bonded over home-cooked meals, honest conversation, glamorous premieres, Miles's storytelling, and Cicely's patient efforts to lessen his dependency on drugs and alcohol. Even so, two years into his relationship with Cicely, Miles married an avant-garde singer 19 years his junior. Devastated and humiliated, Cicely focused on her acting career, winning Oscar nominations and Emmys. Miles's marriage soured within a year.

In their autobiographies, Cicely and Miles wrote about their spiritual connection. Miles marveled at how she could intuit when he was in desperate straits. On Thanksgiving Day, 1981, Cicely and Miles married. Sadly, they did not live happily ever after. Although she accompanied Miles on tours to help him stay sober, he resumed his drug use and philandering, and their union unraveled. As he lay dying in 1991, he asked a mutual friend to tell Cicely he was sorry.

Emilie Blachère

◇

Rémi Ochlik

All that I love you for

2010–2012

The last time Emilie Blachère spoke to her boyfriend, French photojournalist Rémi Ochlik, was on a call from Beirut. It was February 2012, during the anti-government uprising in Syria. Ochlik had already made one trip into the country, and wanted to go back. He had found a way of getting there, he told Emilie, and was seizing the opportunity. After the call, Blachère, a journalist, left for Greece to cover the economic crisis there.

At 28, Rémi had already earned many plaudits for his work. His first major foreign assignment had been in Haiti in 2004, during the overthrow of President Jean-Bertrand Aristide. He had been in the Democratic Republic of Congo in 2008 and had covered the Arab spring in 2011. His photos from Libya won him a prestigious award from the Dutch-based World Press Photo Foundation.

Tragically, Rémi's return journey into Syria in 2012 was to be his last. He made it into the city of Homs, a rebel stronghold under siege by government forces, but on February 22, he and Marie Colvin, an American journalist working for the *The Sunday Times* in London, were killed when a shell smashed into a building that they and other foreign journalists had turned into a makeshift media center.

To commemorate the first anniversary of his death, Emilie posted a love letter to Rémi online. This, she said, was the hardest thing she had ever had to write. All she could think of was his love of making lists of things he wanted, so she decided to list everything she loved about him. She singled out how he would call her

> **❝** I've never found it so difficult to write. My dictionaries are useless. I can already hear you saying, 'Sweet Blachère'. **❞**

Emilie Blachère, 2013

"Blacherounette" when he had something to ask her; how he would make her coffee every morning ("and after eight months, it was actually good"); how he blushed when she told him she was crazy about him; how he would leave love letters for her when he came to feed her cat on days she was away. She described their time together as "magic."

Emilie's "letter" was picked up by the BBC, and she was asked to read it out on a Sunday morning radio program. When Emilie finished reading, the presenter was unable to speak for several seconds. When he did manage to carry on, he was audibly struggling with sobs.

EMILIE BLACHÈRE & RÉMI OCHLIK

Kindred spirits

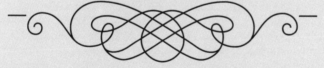

Hojo Masako

◇

Minamoto no Yoritomo

The power of love

1177–1199

Hojo Masako and her husband Minamoto no Yoritomo rose to become one of history's preeminent power couples. Audaciously ambitious and formidably calculating, they established a military government in Japan that ushered in 700 years of samurai rule.

Their origins were humble. Masako was born in 1157 to a minor branch of the Taira warrior clan in rural Izu Province; Yoritomo, ten years her senior, came from a rival clan, the Minamoto. His clan's defeat by the Taira in 1160 led to Yoritomo's banishment to Izu, where the two met, fell in love, and eventually married and had children.

In 1180, Yoritomo raised an army and defeated the Taira, a victory that catapulted him and Masako to national prominence. They established Kamakura, Japan's first warrior capital, and he became its first shogun (military ruler). His vassals recognized her authority, too, even destroying the home of Yoritomo's mistress on Masako's orders.

When Yoritomo died in 1199, Masako became the most powerful person in Kamakura, helping depose her autocratic older son and mentoring his younger brother until his death in 1219. When imperial forces declared war on Kamakura in 1221, Masako rallied the troops by reminding the samurai of the debt they owed her late husband. As she had taken Buddhist vows, Masako is remembered as the "nun shogun."

> **"** Love brought them together but ambition and political savvy helped them transform Japan's political landscape forever. **"**

Ethan Segal, 2021

The Ladies of Llangollen

The chatelaine and the rebel

c. 1778–1829

Ten years before they eloped together, Lady Eleanor Butler and Sarah Ponsonby met through their upper-class Irish families. Sarah was only 13 at the time, and Eleanor 16 years older. Eleanor became Sarah's tutor, and over the years, the two formed a deep intellectual and emotional connection. Prior to the late 19th century, it was common for women to share emotional and even physical intimacy, such as kissing, exchanging love letters, and sleeping in the same bed, and it would generally be considered platonic. No one knows the precise nature of the relationship between Eleanor and Sarah (often called Sally by Eleanor), but they fought to be together and referred to each other in their journals as "my Beloved."

Outside their bond, the women were menaced by their families. Sarah, orphaned at a young age, was subjected to the unwanted sexual advances of her guardian and cousin Sir William Fownes, who was waiting for his wife to die in order to marry her. Eleanor faced censure from her family as an "old maid." Instead of succumbing to these pressures, the women—now 23 and 39—hatched a plan to flee Ireland.

Under the cover of darkness and dressed in men's clothing, the women made for the coast on horseback, to take a ferry across the Irish Sea to Wales. When they missed the ferry, their plan unraveled and their families dragged them home. But the lovers did not give up, and eventually their families allowed them to leave Ireland, taking a maid and enough money to support them.

Lady Eleanor and Sarah in "exquisite retirement"

Eleanor and Sarah settled in rural Llangollen in northeast Wales, establishing their residence at Plas Newydd and enjoying what they called their "exquisite retirement." The Ladies of Llangollen, as the women came to be known, attracted the attention of royalty and famous literary figures, including William Wordsworth, who composed a poem about them. Outside these visits, the women lived in quiet communion, studying languages, reading to each other, writing in their journals, and improving their home. They lived together for more than 50 years.

" How can I acknowledge the kindness and tenderness of my Beloved Sally. "

Lady Eleanor Butler, 1785

Catherine Blake
—◊—
William Blake

Perfect partners

1782–1827

When poet, artist, and engraver William Blake first met his wife, Catherine, he wasn't looking for love; in fact, he had just had his heart broken. While visiting a friend's house one evening, the melancholic William found himself confiding in another guest—19-year-old Catherine Boucher—about his recent romantic misfortune. The empathetic Catherine charmed him, and soon after she became the focus of his affections.

William's father disapproved of the match, unhappy that his son was marrying so young and had chosen the daughter of a market gardener of a lower social class. Nevertheless, William married Catherine in August 1782. Despite her limited education and humble origins, she was in many ways her husband's equal. In addition to running their household alone, Catherine was responsible for buying her husband's paints, ink, and printing materials and managed the household finances. Eventually, she began working alongside him, mixing his colors and printing his engravings, and would color the prints before they were bound and sold.

Catherine also catered to her husband's eccentricities. According to one story, his patron Thomas Butts caught William and Catherine reading *Paradise Lost* together in the nude. When William had one of his visions—which were common—or became frenzied, his wife would stand by his side in silence, offering emotional support. He would later admit that Catherine was the reason many of his works were finished—including his famous Dante series.

> " Stay Kate. Keep just as you are—I will draw your portrait—for you have ever been an angel to me "

William Blake, 1827

A portrait of Catherine by William Blake

Catherine and William were married for almost 45 years. When he fell gravely ill, he thanked her for being an angel to him throughout their life together. After his death on August 12, 1827, Catherine continued to sell his completed works, helping keep her husband's memory alive. She died in 1831.

Simón Bolívar

◆

Manuela Sáenz

The liberator of the liberator

1822–1830

Manuela Sáenz first set eyes on Simón Bolívar in Quito, Ecuador, in June 1822. The president of Gran Colombia, an expanding republic that sought independence from Spain in Latin America, he was known as El Libertador (The Liberator) for his role in leading the revolutions against Spanish rule. He had arrived in Manuela's hometown to celebrate his recent victory over Spanish royalists at the Battle of Pichincha. The pair were introduced at a ball held in his honor, and their intense and illicit relationship began.

Manuela was already married to an Englishman named James Thorne, who unsuccessfully tried to persuade his wife to end the disreputable affair. Although Bolívar felt conflicted about their adultery, he couldn't let go of his beautiful "Manuelita."

The real obstacle to their relationship was distance. Manuela and Bolívar spent most of their time apart, with Bolívar committed to the expansion of Gran Colombia. While Manuela struggled with their prolonged separations, she remained devoted to Bolívar and dedicated herself to the cause of independence.

In 1823, Manuela became Bolívar's personal archivist and was soon one of his closest confidantes. Manuela even saved his life when, in September 1828, she heard conspirators enter his official residence. Waking Bolívar, she convinced him to escape through the bedroom window while she distracted the intruders. From then on, Bolívar was reluctant to be separated from the woman who had risked her life to save his own.

Sadly, the couple were apart when Bolívar died of tuberculosis in 1830. Soon after his death, Gran Colombia collapsed, and Manuela spent the rest of her days in exile in the Peruvian port of Paita, reputedly making a living by selling tobacco. She died during a diphtheria epidemic in 1856. After her death, many historians attempted to erase her name from history. Yet her love for Bolívar became legendary, and she is remembered still as "La Libertadora del Libertador"—the liberator of the liberator.

> " You have made me an idolater ... of Manuela. "
>
> **Simón Bolívar**, 1826

Elizabeth Barrett Browning

$\diamond$

Robert Browning

Poetic soulmates

1846–1861

Months before they met in person, Elizabeth Barrett and Robert Browning cultivated their status as romantic and poetic soulmates in hundreds of love letters. Few relationships have been so deeply rooted in the written word. Their love was buttressed by their shared devotion to books and poetry.

The early lives of Robert and Elizabeth were influenced by parents who were simultaneously doting and domineering. Ba, the family's pet name for Elizabeth, was the eldest of 12 children. She spent her idyllic early childhood years at Hope End, her family's country estate in Herefordshire, England. At 15, Barrett contracted an unspecified, debilitating illness that was to affect her for the rest of her life. For her pain and nervous symptoms, she was prescribed laudanum, a tincture of opium, which became a lifelong habit that she assiduously defended to her dubious husband. During a period of poetic inspiration, she once stated that she longed to live alone in a forest, alternately taking opium and writing poems.

Robert Browning was the son of an abolitionist bank clerk who gave up the chance of a lucrative career in the family's sugar business due to his opposition to slavery. Robert's first and only ambition was to be a poet. His early published works, such as *Sordello* (1840), met with a mixed reception, but Elizabeth, whose publications included *The Seraphim and Other Poems* (1838) and a two-volume collection, *Poems* (1844), defended his work. Writing to thank her in 1845, Robert seemed to have fallen in love merely by reading her work: "I do, as I say, love these books with all my heart—and I love you too."

> " By tomorrow at this time,
> I shall have you only,
> to love me—my beloved! "

Elizabeth Barrett Browning, 1846

By the time Robert began his courtship in earnest, the Barrett family had suffered financial reversals, although they were still well-to-do— Elizabeth having received a bequest from a wealthy aunt. The family moved to a large house on Wimpole Street in London, where Elizabeth, whose health was still delicate, was largely confined to her bedroom and a small sitting room. Undaunted by the bitter opposition of her father, and the fact that she was 39 years old (six years older than him), Robert pursued her ardently, visiting Wimpole Street some 91 times.

Robert and Elizabeth exchanged near daily letters, writing even on days when they saw each other. Their correspondence discussed books; commented on each other's work; gossiped about literary lights of the day, such as Wordsworth and Tennyson; and slowly built

Robert and Elizabeth with Flush at Wimpole Street

" O' Lyric Love, half angel and half bird,
And all a wonder and a wild desire "

Robert Browning, 1868

their trust and delight in each other. The letters are models of true conversation between two compatible individuals. By the time they make their plans to elope, readers of the letters can only cheer.

The couple's elopement in September 1846 was accomplished with the help of Elizabeth's faithful maid. While her family was out, Elizabeth stole away to Marylebone Parish Church and married Robert, with only the maid and Robert's cousin, James Silverthorne, as witnesses. Elizabeth then returned to Wimpole Street and kept the marriage secret for a week, until the couple's final getaway (with her maid and spaniel, Flush, in tow).

The lovers honeymooned in Paris and then traveled on to Italy, settling in Florence, in an elegant apartment near the Pitti Palace and Boboli Gardens. They established a salon there, welcoming British poet Walter Savage Landor and writer and feminist Fanny Trollope. Elizabeth befriended her Scottish neighbors, the Ogilvy family. Eliza Ogilvy, the matriarch, also a published poet, was with Elizabeth when she gave birth to her son, Robert ("Pen") Browning, at the age of 43.

Both Brownings found Florence an inspiration to their poetry: in 1856, Elizabeth published *Aurora Leigh*, a long poem with a Florentine heroine; Robert reveled in Renaissance art, and wrote dramatic monologues centered on artists such as Andrea del Sarto and Fra Lippo Lippi. After 15 years of joyful and productive life together, Elizabeth's health finally failed in 1861; her final word to her husband was a murmured "beautiful."

Sonnets from the Portuguese

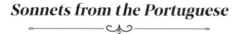

In 1849, Elizabeth presented Robert with a packet of 44 sonnets that she had written during the course of their courtship. Published in 1850, *Sonnets from the Portuguese* (the title is a reference to Robert's playful name for his dark-haired wife) are heartfelt expressions of the development of deep love. Although they may not live up to Robert's praise as the finest sonnet sequence since Shakespeare, they were widely acclaimed and their reputation has endured. Sonnet 43 begins with the often quoted line: "How do I love thee? Let me count the ways."

Jane Addams

◇

Mary Rozet Smith

The reformer and the philanthropist

1890–1934

❝ You must know, dear, how
I long for you all the time ...
There is reason in the habit of
married folk keeping together. **❞**

Jane Addams, 1902

K nown today as the "mother of social work," as well as the first American woman to win a Nobel Peace Prize (1931), Jane Addams lived an extraordinary life of progressive activism and public service. In 1889, she founded Hull House in Chicago with her then-partner Ellen Gates Starr. Women working at Hull House developed and distributed social services to recently arrived immigrants in the city.

Soon after its founding, wealthy philanthropist Mary Rozet Smith visited Hull House and met Jane. A friendship developed, and by 1892 Jane had parted from Ellen and formed a relationship with Mary.

The two women spent more than 35 years together, with Mary acting as Jane's secretary and confidante while Jane campaigned against child labor laws, advocated women's suffrage and pacifism in World War I, and supported the National Association for the Advancement of Colored People. The two women traveled across the US and Europe together. Upon Mary's death in 1934, Jane wrote to her nephew, "I suppose I could have willed my heart to stop beating, but the thought of what she had been to me for so long kept me from being cowardly."

Mary Rozet Smith (left) and Jane Addams *c.* 1896

Emilie Flöge
◇
Gustav Klimt

The painter and the muse

1887–1916

Austrian painter Gustav Klimt first met the Flöge family when he and his brother Ernst painted the three Flöge daughters as subjects for a theater project. Ernst later married the middle sister, Helene Flöge, and when Ernst died in 1892, leaving Helene pregnant, Gustav helped his sister-in-law financially and became guardian to her child. The family often welcomed Gustav into their home in Vienna and spent summers with him at Lake Attersee. Their youngest daughter Emilie was in her late teens at the time—12 years Klimt's junior.

Emilie became one of Gustav's principal models, serving as his lifelong muse and creative partner. She was a member of Viennese bohemian circles, together with Helene and older sister Pauline, who was an avant-garde fashion designer. In 1904, the Flöge sisters opened a fashion house called the Schwestern Flöge, famous for creating a boldly printed version of the "Reform dress," a long, flowing gown that offered women freedom from corsets. Some of the elite women Gustav painted posed in Emilie's designs.

By all accounts, Emilie and Gustav's relationship was one of intellectual equals, but historians still debate its exact nature. He was a notorious womanizer who conceived 14 children with various women without marrying any of them. When Gustav died from a stroke at age 55, he left one half of his estate to his family, and the other to Emilie. When Emilie herself died in 1952, some 400 postcards and letters from Gustav were found among her possessions, but her responses do not survive to throw light on their relationship.

Emilie Flöge, painted by Klimt in 1902

" Look attentively at my
pictures and there recognize
what I am and what I want. "

Gustav Klimt, 1900

Marie Curie

—•———•———•—

Pierre Curie

Perfect chemistry

1895–1906

❝ We were made to live together and our union had to be. ❞

Marie Curie, 1906

Marie and Pierre at work in their laboratory

M arie Skłodowska, a 26-year-old Polish student scraping by in Paris, and Pierre Curie, a French scientist, initially resisted the magnetic pull of their mutual attraction when they met in 1894. They had both intended to remain solitary, devoting themselves to science. Pierre, 35, still lived at home with his parents.

There is a homeliness to the details of their love affair. Their honeymoon in 1895 was a bicycle trip around the French countryside, and Marie's wedding gown was a plain blue dress she specified must be reusable for lab work. The laboratory where they pursued their research into radioactivity, resulting in the 1903 Nobel Prize for Physics, was an old wooden hangar that was barely more than a stable.

Their partnership lasted just 11 years. In 1906, Pierre was trampled to death under the wheels of a carriage. After Pierre's death, Marie began a diary in which she wrote to him as though he were still alive. She told him she sought refuge in their laboratory, but that the beloved shabby space "had an infinite silence and seemed a desert."

Nadezhda Mandelstam

◆

Osip Mandelstam

True to love's legacy

1919–1938

Nothing ever shook Nadezhda Khazina's determination to preserve the legacy of her husband, Osip Mandelstam—not even Stalinist tyranny. When the couple met in Kiev in 1919, Mandelstam was already one of Russia's outstanding poets. They married in 1922 and lived in Moscow, the leading lights of a literary and intellectual circle.

Celebrity did not guarantee safety under the Stalinist regime, and in 1934, Osip was taken to Lubyanka prison, where his interrogators produced a satirical poem he had written about Stalin. As Osip had only ever recited the poem to friends, it seemed that one them must have betrayed him. When Osip was condemned to three years' exile in the Urals, Nadezhda chose to accompany him. After he tried to jump out of a window, the sentence was made less harsh, and the couple were allowed to live anywhere in the Soviet Union, apart from its 12 largest cities. They chose Voronezh in the southwest, where Osip wrote what would become known as his *Voronezh Notebook* poems.

The Stalinist purges intensified, and in 1938 Osip was arrested and condemned to a Gulag labor camp. He got as far as a transit camp, where he died, officially of heart failure. For Nadezhda, her life now had one overriding goal—to preserve her husband's poetry. She memorized his unpublished poems, for fear that any transcripts would be destroyed if she were arrested. During the 1960s and '70s, she published the later poems clandestinely and wrote two volumes of memoirs. Nadezhda died in 1980, having achieved her aim—to keep the work of one of the 20th century's greatest poets safe.

Lorena Hickok

Eleanor Roosevelt

The journalist and the social reformer

1932–1962

I n 1932, Associated Press reporter Lorena Hickok was assigned the task of writing about the activities of First Lady Eleanor Roosevelt, wife of Franklin D. Roosevelt, the 32nd President of the United States. The two women quickly became close. Eleanor invited Lorena—called "Hick" by friends—to ride in her private car, attend shows with her, and join her for dinner. Hick, aware that this intimacy compromised her responsibilities as a journalist, left the Associated Press the following year. In Roosevelt's third term (1941–1945) as president, Hick moved into the White House. The press referred to her as Eleanor's companion.

Over the three decades Hick and Eleanor were together—right up until Eleanor's death in 1962—they exchanged almost 4,000 letters, sometimes writing two letters a day. Eleanor referred to Hick in her letters as "my darling," "dear one," and "light of my life," and the women would frequently speak of their longing to reunite when they had to be apart. In August, 1934, Hick wrote to Eleanor, "At times life becomes just one long, dreary ache for you." While their passion waned over time, particularly after World War II, their tenderness never died.

Vita Sackville–West

◇

Virginia Woolf

A slow burn

1922–1929

When English poet and novelist Vita Sackville-West first met fellow English writer Virginia Woolf in December 1922, she was electrified by Virginia's mind and presence. Four days later, after she had invited Virginia to her home in London, Vita wrote in a letter to her husband, "Darling, I have quite lost my heart."

Vita sought to get to know Virginia better, talking to her at dinner parties and meeting her for lunch. Their relationship progressed slowly and intimately, first as friends—when they called each other Mrs. Woolf and Mrs. Nicolson (Vita's married name)—then from 1925 as lovers. The physical attraction had been building for some time. In a diary entry of 1924, Virginia confided that Vita "has no very sharp brain. But as a body hers is perfection," adding that Vita was "in short (what I have never been) a real woman." Both women were married to men, but this didn't stop them being together.

Vita was Virginia's inspiration for her trailblazing 1928 novel *Orlando,* which explores the fluidity of gender and sexuality. Scholars have described *Orlando* as Virginia's love letter to Vita in novel form: it is dedicated to Vita and includes a photograph of her. By then, however, Vita had fallen in love with Mary Campbell, the wife of South African poet Roy Campbell, and her affair with Virginia was drawing to a close. In September 1928, just before *Orlando*'s publication, Vita and Virginia took their only holiday together, in France. Although they enjoyed the holiday, their love was transforming into friendship, which lasted until Virginia's death by suicide in 1941.

" Somewhere I have seen a
little ball bubbling up and
down on the spray of a fountain:
the fountain is you; the ball me. "

Virginia Woolf, 1928

Simone de Beauvoir

Jean-Paul Sartre

Mostly in the mind

1929–1980

Simone de Beauvoir and Jean-Paul Sartre became lovers as students in Paris in 1929. Aged 21 and 24 respectively, they were both studying philosophy, he at the École Normale Supérieure and she at the Sorbonne. They would go on to become two of the most important philosophers of their generation. Simone's 1949 classic *The Second Sex* prefigured the second-wave feminist movement, while Jean-Paul's *Being and Nothingness*, published in 1943, introduced existentialism.

Simone and Jean-Paul's open relationship was unconventional for the time. Jean-Paul proposed a "pact" in which they could pursue other relationships providing they told each other everything. Simone agreed, although she would struggle with jealousy. So began decades of the pair searching for sexual partners outside their relationship, including young women selected from Simone's students. The couple would regularly conspire to have sex with the same women or their sisters, lying to those involved and writing each other detailed, and often cruel, accounts of their escapades. When these letters were published years after their deaths, those they had seduced expressed shock and betrayal.

In the late 1940s, Jean-Paul stopped being sexually intimate with Simone. Although they never lived together and never married, they maintained their connection until Jean-Paul's death in 1980. When Simone died in 1986, her ashes were interred at Montparnasse Cemetery, joining the remains of Jean-Paul.

Charles Eames

◆

Ray Eames

Perfect symmetry

1940–1978

This husband-and-wife design duo lived in a glass house overlooking the Pacific Ocean in California. The exterior of the house, an elegant and functional shoebox of glass and steel, was Charles; the interior, full of plants; color; and playful touches, such as paintings hung on the ceiling to contemplate from the sofa, was Ray. Together, the couple created a new style for the postwar era. Their aim, in Charles's words, was "to make the best for the most for the least."

For the Eameses, work was play, and they dubbed their office in Venice, California, a laboratory of ideas. Everything they did from the plywood splint for soldiers wounded in World War II to the Eames chairs in molded plywood was an instant design classic. Charles once remarked, "Anything I can do, Ray can do better," but in the 1950s, he was seen as the more important member of their partnership. The symmetry apparent in their work was mirrored at the end; Ray died ten years to the day after Charles. In the period after his death, she finished the projects they had begun together and cataloged their life's work.

Ruby Hunter

—◊—

Archie Roach

Let love rule

1971–2010

Serendipity brought Aboriginal Australian singer-songwriters Archie Roach and Ruby Hunter together. In 1973, a toss of a coin led Archie to hitchhike to Adelaide, where he met Ruby at a Salvation Army hostel. He was 15, Ruby 16. Archie was reserved, Ruby the talker. The pair became good friends. They both belonged to Australia's Stolen Generation—Indigenous children forcibly taken from their families by the state and raised in institutions and foster families. Ruby had been living on the streets for a year after leaving a home for "troubled" girls.

More hopeful in Ruby's presence, Archie started playing music. They shared an intense connection, and when Archie moved back to Melbourne to find his family, Ruby soon followed. The moment he and Ruby saw one another again, they shared their first kiss.

Archie and Ruby spent their days working casual jobs, and their nights dancing and singing. The couple moved around, but they were both dogged by alcoholism, especially Archie. Eventually, after 15 years together, Ruby left Archie, and this was the spur that made him turn his life around. The couple reunited, and the pair began to make names for themselves as singer-songwriters. In 1988, Ruby performed her song "Proud, Proud Woman" at a festival in Sydney; in 1990, Archie was offered the opportunity to record an album. When Archie expressed reluctance to accept the offer, Ruby uttered words he would never forget, "It's not all about you Archie Roach." The album, *Charcoal Road*, includes Archie's masterpiece "Took the Children Away" and the song "Down City Streets," which was written by Ruby.

Ruby and Archie performing in Sydney in 2008

The lifelong collaborators went on to achieve individual and joint success in Australia and internationally. With Ruby's health deteriorating in the 2000s, the pair spent most of their time at home, surrounded by family. In 2010, Archie's soulmate of four decades died of a heart attack, at the age of 54. Archie struggled to cope, yet Ruby's memory got him through his darkest time: when he stopped shaving and leaving the house, he heard her voice: "Just take a look at yourself Archie Roach … go and clean yourself up." Ruby had gone, but the healing power of her spirit remained.

" I hadn't talked much to anybody, and she just had this way … she just had this personality that endeared you to her. "

Archie Roach, 2020

Enduring love

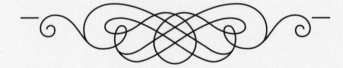

Khnumhotep
Niankhkhnum

Overseers of the palace manicurists

c. 2380–2320 BCE

Khnumhotep and Niankhkhnum supervised the manicurists to the king during the Fifth Dynasty of ancient Egypt's Old Kingdom. Clues about the lives of these two men emerged in 1964 when archaeologists unearthed their joint burial tomb in the ancient city of Saqqara, 9 miles (15 km) south of the pyramids at Giza. The multi-room burial chambers include wall paintings of the two holding hands and embracing nose-to-nose, their belts touching as they look into each other's eyes. The intimacy shown is similar to that typically found in a tomb for a husband and wife, leading some scholars to think that Khnumhotep and Niankhkhnum were a same-sex couple. If this is true, their tomb would be the earliest known evidence of a same-sex relationship.

Both men had wives and children—possibly because of the importance of lineage in ancient Egypt—but the wives play only a minor role in the paintings. A banquet scene in which Niankhkhnum's wife Khentikaus originally embraced her husband as an honored guest was removed by the tomb artists, leaving only a faint outline. In one scene, Khnumhotep is depicted smelling a lotus flower, an act almost exclusively associated with women in Fifth Dynasty art. This could point to Khnumhotep having the symbolic status of a wife.

Given that the tomb is the only information archaeologists have about Khnumhotep and Niankhkhnum, historians may never know the real nature of their relationship or their life, but clearly the men wished to be remembered together.

Justinian

— ◇ —

Theodora

For love and empire

c. 520–548 CE

Justinian, the future emperor of the Eastern Roman Empire, is thought to have met his wife, Theodora, in around 520, while she was working as an actress. From the outset, their relationship was controversial, as actresses were forbidden by law from marrying anyone of noble rank. Justinian successfully convinced his uncle, Emperor Justin I, to revoke the law, but the couple did not marry until 525 CE, after the death of the disapproving Empress Euphemia, the wife of Justin I. Two years later, Justinian ascended the throne.

Justinian considered Theodora his political equal and coruler; anyone swearing an oath to him had to make the same promise to her. She offered her husband unparalleled support during the Nika revolt in Constantinople in 532, convincing her husband to confront the rebels rather than abandon the city. She was also charitable and pious, commissioning churches, improving the lives of women and the poor, and building hospitals. The couple worked side by side until Theodora's death in 548. Heartbroken, Justinian ruled alone until his death in 565.

Abigail Adams

---❦---

John Adams

A lifelong congress

1762–1804

John Adams, a 24-year old lawyer from Braintree, Massachusetts, met 15-year-old Abigail Smith, who would later become his wife, in the parlor of her parents' house in 1759. John was a Harvard graduate, while Abigail was unschooled, though not unlettered. In the early years of their marriage, he teased Abigail for her "habit of reading, writing, and thinking."

From the start of their relationship and right through their marriage, John and Abigail wrote to one another whenever they were apart. The series of 1,160 extant letters begins on October 4, 1762, with "Miss Adorable" and ends more than 39 years later in February 1801 with "Adieu my dear Friend." It bookended their dramatic lives during the American Revolution and the country's early years of independence from Britain.

John Adams was one of the leaders in the struggle for American independence. He played prominent roles in the Continental Congress (the governing body of the rebel colonies and later of the United States) and helped draft the Declaration of Independence. When he was far from home, the wisest and most pertinent advice always came from the pen of Abigail, who was bringing up their children and managing the farm in Braintree. He wrote to her every morning, before the Congressional sessions began; she wrote to him every evening, after the children had gone to bed. Her letters were full of news from the home front. In June 1775, she described the noise and smoke of the Battle of Bunker Hill, 10 miles (16 km) away.

Beginning in 1778, John Adams spent the best part of a decade abroad, mostly in France and Holland, negotiating loans, treaties of assistance, and finally the 1783 Treaty of Paris, which ended the war.

> " Miss Adorable ... I presume I have good Right to draw upon you for the Kisses as I have given two or three Millions at least. "

John Adams, 1762

All that time, Abigail would write each night from Braintree. After the peace, she joined him in Paris, gliding effortlessly through Versailles, the most opulent court in Europe, and meeting Louis XVI and Marie Antoinette. She was not so well-received in London, where her husband was the first American minister to the Court of St. James, perhaps because she was too vigorously American for British tastes.

While John could be brooding, Abigail was sunny and optimistic. He was always her "dearest friend." He called her his "ballast," and her even temper kept his more volatile disposition in check, especially during the years when he was Vice President to George Washington and then Second President of the United States. As the first "First Lady," she was John's official hostess and chief advisor, first in Philadelphia and later in the unfinished White House in Washington, D.C., a city that was then a muddy construction site.

In 1800, President Adams lost his reelection bid in the narrowest of contests against Thomas Jefferson. Accompanied by his "dearest friend," he returned to Braintree (now Quincy), where he enjoyed swinging a scythe in his own fields, Abigail often by his side. On October 28, 1818, Abigail died of typhoid fever. Not only had she been the wife of one Chief Executive, but she would also go down in history as the mother of another—in 1825, John saw their eldest son, John Quincy Adams, elected as the Sixth President of the United States. A year later on July 4, 1826, John Adams himself died, on the same day as Thomas Jefferson.

Homekeeper, bookkeeper, and entrepreneur

Left to her own devices for long stretches of time, Abigail managed the family finances, invested in bonds, and bought property on the Canadian border. She also sold items made scarce by war shortages. Spotting that pins were in short supply in Massachusetts in 1776, she instructed John to send a "bundle" (6,000) from Philadelphia that she could sell and barter. Later, when John was in Europe, she asked him to send trunk loads of luxury items, such as handkerchiefs and ribbons, telling her husband that such small items had the best profit.

Portraits of Abigail Adams and her husband John

" Should I draw you the picture
of my heart, it would be what I
hope you still would love, though
it contained nothing new. "

Abigail Adams, 1782

Johann Wolfgang von Goethe

◇

Christiane Vulpius

Defying social norms

1788–1816

Johann Wolfgang von Goethe, author of *The Sorrows of Young Werther*—the story of a young man driven to suicide—was one of the most famous writers in Germany, but he chose a woman society deemed beneath him. Before becoming Johann's mistress, Christiane Vulpius had worked in a factory making artificial flowers. Society was shocked when Johann brought the pregnant girl to live openly in his house.

What people disdained in Christiane—plump good looks, a smiling simplicity, housewifely skills—Johann adored, calling her his "house treasure." Christiane further enriched his life by giving him a son, August, on Christmas Day, 1789. Yet Johann did not marry her for another 17 years.

Johann overcame his deep-seated fear of marriage and commitment only after Christiane defended his house and property from plunder by Napoleon's soldiers after the Battle of Jena, which took place 10 miles (16 km) from Weimar in 1806. The couple married five days afterward. When Christiane died ten years later, Johann wrote, "The whole gain of my life is to lament her loss."

Charity Bryant

Sylvia Drake

Two minds united in one

1807–1851

When 29-year-old Charity Bryant visited her cousin in Weymouth, Vermont, in February 1807, she thought the trip would be brief, a peaceful break from the pressures of her life as a teacher working in various Massachusetts towns.

It was during the trip to Weymouth that Charity first laid eyes on her cousin's charming sister-in-law, Sylvia Drake. The spark between the two women led to 44 years together—the rest of Charity's life. An independent 22-year-old, Sylvia was very different from the ideal image of womanhood in 19th-century rural New England. She preferred books and poetry to domestic life, and refused to marry any of the men who tried to court her. Charity, a talented seamstress as well as a teacher, hired Sylvia as her assistant. Within a few months, the two women had moved into a one-bedroom apartment in Weymouth. They would always celebrate this day, July 3, as their anniversary.

Charity and Sylvia built a flourishing tailoring business that earned them the respect of the local community. Townsfolk quietly looked upon them as a married couple, calling them "Aunt Charity" and "Aunt Sylvia." Charity's nephew, William Cullen Bryant, called their union "no less sacred to them than the tie of marriage." Upon Charity's death in 1851, Sylvia wore a widow's black mourning dress until her own death 16 years later. The couple's shared grave can be visited to this day in the little Vermont town where they fell in love more than 200 years ago.

Juliette Drouet

·——◆——·

Victor Hugo

A literary love affair

1833–1883

" In all the beauty that surrounds me, I recognize you. Beautiful forms, beautiful colors, smooth perfumes, harmonious sounds, all of these mean you to me. **"**

Juliette Drouet, 1835

Juliette Drouet, c.1827

French poet, novelist, and playwright Victor Hugo, author of the epic novel *Les Misérables*, was a man with a voracious sexual appetite, whose numerous affairs continued almost until his death at 83. Yet his most remarkable relationship, with one-time actress Juliette Drouet, was especially close and lasted for 50 years. They met when she played a minor role in his play *Lucrèce Borgia*. Their first night together, on February 16, 1833, is commemorated in *Les Misérables* as the wedding night of Marius and Cosette.

Victor had fame and wealth and, at 31, was married with three children; Juliette became his secretary, transcribing and editing his work. When he had to flee France in 1851, due to his opposition to Louis Napoléon (later Napoleon III), Juliette organized the production of false papers. She followed him to Brussels with a trunk full of his work. After Brussels, Victor lived on the Channel Islands of Jersey and Guernsey. In Guernsey, he and his wife Adèle occupied one house and Juliette another nearby. After Adèle's death in 1868, Juliette and Victor lived together in Paris. Juliette died in 1883; he two years later.

Anne Lister

◇

Ann Walker

Rebels with a cause

1834–1840

Born into a comfortable landowning family in Yorkshire, England, in 1791, Anne Lister began having relationships with other women at boarding school. Her diary—started when she was 15 and ultimately containing more than four million words—was partially written in code, which included algebraic notations and symbols of the zodiac. Historians would later discover that this code contained details about her sex life. It is one of the earliest and most detailed first-hand accounts of sex between women in Western Europe.

Anne attracted attention for wearing masculine clothing and top hats—earning her the nickname "Gentleman Jack" and stoking local gossip—and for her business activities, such as buying a local mine. As a young woman, her great love was Mariana Belcombe, but Mariana was reluctant to expose herself to the public ridicule directed at Anne and married a wealthy landowning man in 1816.

Heartbroken, Anne resolved to find someone else to share her life. Sixteen years later, at the age of 40, she began pursuing Ann Walker, a wealthy local heiress. Shy and 11 years her junior, Walker faced mental health battles that would likely be classified as anxiety and depression today. Using all her flirtatious charms, Anne wooed Walker on long country walks, and two years later persuaded her to move into Shibden Hall, the Lister family estate. On March 30, 1834, the women exchanged rings, made lifelong pledges to each other, and took communion together in church. They considered this date to be their wedding anniversary.

The couple renovated Shibden Hall (using Ann's money) and traveled extensively together. But six years later, in September 1840, while traveling through Russia and Astrakhan (now Georgia), Anne died when an insect bite turned septic. Ann returned to Shibden Hall to wait for Anne's embalmed body, which did not arrive until April. Tragically, Ann's brother-in-law forcibly removed Ann from Shibden Hall in 1843 when he had her declared insane and sent to an asylum for a time. Ann died at her family home in 1854, at the age of 50.

> 66 If she will bind herself so that I can have confidence, I hope and think we shall get on together happily. 99

Anne Lister, 1834

Prince Albert

Queen Victoria

The loving and the beloved

1839–1861

When 20-year old Prince Albert of Saxe-Coburg-Gotha in central Germany arrived at Windsor Castle in October 1839, it was only the second time he had laid eyes on the young Queen Victoria. They were first cousins, born three months apart, and she had recently acceded to the throne of Great Britain and Ireland. The meeting had been arranged by older members of their intertwined families. Five days later, she asked the handsome prince to marry her, as befitted her station. He bowed and accepted, and the pair were married in St. James's Palace in London in February 1840.

Victoria was queen not just of Britain but of a vast empire. She wanted her husband to have a role, and Albert needed an outlet for his energies. A born reformer, he organized and streamlined the royal household and planned in great detail the education of their nine children. There were some difficult moments: Victoria could be emotionally volatile; he could be severe. But bonds of deep affection grew and strengthened, and the Queen increasingly depended on Albert's wisdom, guidance, and able management.

Prince Albert had vision and saw possibilities. Concerned by the lagging state of industry and manufacturing in Britain, he instigated the 1851 Great Exhibition, an international display of 14,000 scientific and technological exhibits in the Crystal Palace, an enormous glass-paneled building put up in London's Hyde Park. Its success spurred advances in British trade and industry, and profits from the event paid for a site in South Kensington dedicated to the arts and sciences, centering on what is now the Victoria and Albert Museum.

Albert also occupied himself with matters of government, laboring over state papers long into the night. During the Crimean War with Russia in 1854–1856, he helped devise British strategy. He was now a king in all but name, and on June 25, 1857, Victoria gave him the title "Prince Consort."

Perhaps Albert worked himself too hard, or perhaps he ignored the symptoms, but in 1861 he was diagnosed with typhoid fever. On December 14, 1861, he died in Windsor Castle at the age of 42. Queen Victoria was devastated, and the shadow of that tragedy stalked her

> " He clasped me in his arms, & we kissed each other again & again! His beauty, his sweetness & gentleness—really how can I ever be thankful enough to have such a Husband! "

Queen Victoria, 1840

for the rest of her life. For the next 40 years, she dressed in black. The memory of Albert never faded. Albert's suite of rooms at Windsor remained untouched, and fresh clothing was laid out for Albert each morning. "Dear Albert" remained a feature of her conversation, a name soon strewn across the British empire in place names and monuments. In London alone, there is the Albert Bridge; the Albert Embankment; the Albert Gate; and two lavish monuments, years in the making: the Albert Hall, an auditorium beneath a vast glass-and-iron dome, and the Albert Memorial, featuring a statue of the prince, surrounded by an array of allegorical figures, and holding the catalog of the Great Exhibition.

Victoria and Albert are buried in the royal mausoleum at Frogmore, outside Windsor Castle. The royal couple had begun planning a tomb for themselves even before Albert died. Four days after his death, she chose the site and work began a few weeks later. By 1871, when the final stone was placed, an exquisite Byzantine-style monument had arisen, its interior shimmering with mosaics, its central dome above the royal sarcophagus.

Victoria reigned for 40 more years after Albert's death. By the end of her 63-year reign, the empire encompassed a quarter of the world's population and the Victorian Era, as it became known, was one of unprecedented economic prosperity in Britain. When Victoria died on January 22 1901, her body was placed in the mausoleum arrayed in a white dress and wearing her wedding veil.

The wedding dress

Queen Victoria popularized bridal white in Europe and America. Until then, brides who could afford it wore a brightly colored dresses while poor women put on the best dress they owned. After Victoria's wedding, white was seen as a sign of affluence and came to denote virginity. It was not until the mid-20th century, when clothes became cheaper to produce, that the middle and lower classes could afford to follow suit. The long, white dress has since caught on in countries outside the West, though brides in India often wear red, as do traditional brides in China, where red symbolizes good luck.

> " To be cut off in the prime of life ...
> when I had hoped with such instinctive
> certainty that God never would part us,
> and would let us grow old together ...
> is too awful, too cruel! "

Queen Victoria, 1861

Queen Victoria on Her Wedding Day by Franz Xaver Winterhalter

Charles Stratton

◇

Lavinia Warren Stratton

Mr. and Mrs. Tom Thumb

1863–1883

“ The General honestly kissed his wife, and ... bestowed upon her the 'killing glance' with which he once captivated so many damsels. **”**

The New York Times, 1863

The happy couple on their wedding day in 1863

When Charles Stratton was a child, American circus magnate P. T. Barnum approached his family with a view to putting Charles, who had dwarfism, in his freak show. Shows such as these were popular at the time, although they would now be considered offensive. Charles left his family in Bridgeport, Connecticut, to tour with Barnum and went on to have a lucrative career as "General Tom Thumb."

In 1862, Lavinia Warren, a fellow performer with dwarfism, joined Barnum's "living museum" of people with unusual physical attributes. Charles and Lavinia fell in love and married the following year, in what was described by the press as a "fairy wedding" with 2,000 guests. Charles and Lavinia spent 20 years together. Eventually retiring from public performances, they traveled the world, meeting famous people such as Abraham Lincoln and Mary Todd Lincoln, Queen Victoria, and Pope Pius IX. Despite often being treated in a condescending manner, they lived comfortably. Charles spent his wealth lavishly, leaving Lavinia only remnants of their fortune when he died in 1883, aged 45.

Lavinia married again, to fellow performer Count Primo Magri. Yet when she died in 1919, at the age of 78, Lavinia was buried next to Charles, forever faithful to the love of her life.

Gertrude Stein

Alice B. Toklas

The vanguard of the avant-garde

1907–1946

The first encounter of Gertrude Stein and Alice B. Toklas was a meeting of minds. Gertrude was a writer and Alice a pianist, and they both loved art and Paris. Once they met, the pair became so entwined that Gertrude referred to them as "Gertrice" or "Altrude."

Alice and Gertrude were brought together by the consequences of a natural disaster. In 1906, Alice was living in San Francisco when an earthquake devastated the city. The quake brought Michael and Sarah Stein, Gertrude's eldest brother and his wife, back from Paris, so they could check on their property. While there, they told their neighbor, Alice, all about their lives in Paris. Alice, entranced by their description, moved to Paris the following year.

At the time, Gertrude Stein was living in Paris, in the rue de Fleurus, with her brother Leo. The pair were very close, and were making names for themselves as art collectors. Their purchase of Henri Matisse's *Woman with a Hat* in 1905 helped launch the artist's career. But at 33 years old, Gertrude was living in Leo's shadow. He was not supportive of her writing, and she was lonely.

When Alice arrived in Paris in 1907, Gertrude decided to welcome her, as a favor to Michael—whose business dealings helped fund the lives of all of his siblings. On a fateful walk together, the women immediately recognized each other as kindred spirits. Alice became indispensable to Gertrude, encouraging her avant-garde writing where Leo had not, and visiting her at home, where she would type up Gertrude's manuscripts and drink coffee.

The relationship remained platonic until around 1910, when Gertrude "proposed" to Alice. After this, the two were certainly lovers. Alice moved into the rue de Fleurus. Their relationship encouraged Gertrude to explore gender and sexuality in her writing, but the women avoided associating with Paris's lesbian circles, which had a scandalous reputation.

When World War I came, Gertrude and Alice did what they could for the war effort. They volunteered with the American Fund for French Wounded, and traveled together in Gertrude's car, "Auntie," delivering soldiers to the front line or back to their billets, and transporting supplies. They would later note that the only real arguments they ever had were over Gertrude's bad driving.

Once the war ended in 1918, their literary and artistic lives resumed. Gertrude's star was on the rise, and Paris was attracting more and more American and British writers and artists, many of whom flocked to the rue de Fleurus.

" In the morning there is meaning, in the evening there is feeling. "

Gertrude Stein, 1914

Gertrude and Alice spent the roaring twenties quietly, content with the company of each other and their poodle, Basket. They were still inseparable—so much so, that in 1933 Gertrude published *The Autobiography of Alice B. Toklas,* the story of their life together told from Alice's point of view, in Alice's voice. The book would make both women household names, and stand as a testament to how intimately they knew each other.

By the time World War II broke out, Alice and Gertrude were in their sixties. Rather than flee France after the Nazis reached Paris, the pair moved to their country house in a small southern village. Despite being well known as both lesbians and Jews, they escaped persecution under the Nazi regime. It was probably Gertrude's friendship with a Vichy government officer named Bernard Faÿ that kept them safe—and stopped the Nazis from looting their art collection.

The women survived two world wars, only for Gertrude to pass away from stomach cancer in 1946, at the age of 72. She had spent nearly 40 years at Alice's side, and now Alice was left alone. She published cookbooks, including *The Alice B. Toklas Cookbook* (1954), mixing recipes with reminiscences and including her recipe for hashish fudge. In her final years, Alice's sight failed and she was unable to see the paintings she and Gertrude had collected. The rest of her life would be dedicated to her partner's memory, until she died in 1967 at the age of 89. After 21 years apart, Alice and Gertrude were reunited in Paris's Père Lachaise cemetery, with a shared grave and headstone.

A Paris salon

Gertrude and Alice's home, at 27 rue de Fleurus, was part art gallery and part meeting place for artists and writers, such as Matisse (left), Picasso, and Hemingway. With Alice curating, the salon hosted invitation-only events on Saturday evenings, when Gertrude and Alice would play husband and wife: Gertrude would talk with the (mostly all) male writers and artists, while Alice cooked elaborate meals and entertained their wives.

> **" Gertrude has said things tonight it will take her 10 years to understand. "**
>
> **Alice B. Toklas**

Alice B. Toklas (left) and Gertrude Stein with Basket, c. 1944

Clementine Churchill

—◇—

Winston Churchill

Pug and Pussy

1908–1965

> **❝** Sweet cat—I kiss your vision as it rises before my mind. Your dear heart throbs often in my own. **❞**

Winston Churchill, 1909

Clementine and Winston, 1944

In March 1908, Clementine Hozier, then 22, received an invitation to a dinner party at her aunt's house. She was a last-minute addition to make 14 guests, as 13 would have been unlucky. Sitting next to her was Winston Churchill, a junior government minister nearly a decade older. The two had met before, at a ball in 1904, but this time they clicked. They married within six months and went on to have five children. The fourth died at the age of two, a tragedy they bore together.

Winston rose to high office, with Clementine providing advice and support. Although Winston's focus on his career came at the expense of time with Clementine, the affection and respect between them was evident. They nicknamed each other "pussy" and "pug" (or "pig") and often greeted each other with meowing and woofing.

During World War II, when Winston was helping lead the fight against fascism, Clementine was one of the few people who would challenge him, privately admonishing him to be kinder to his staff. Winston's death in 1965—following prolonged ill-health—brought an end to a loving union that had lasted more than 56 years.

Marc Chagall

◆————◆————◆

Bella Rosenfeld

The flying lovers of Vitebsk

1914–1944

Mark Chagall's art tells movingly of his love for his wife, Bella Rosenfeld. Painting after painting depicts her as a symbol of love and vitality. Among the most haunting are works such as *Birthday* (1915), in which the couple fly, dreamlike, above the ground, as if the power of their passion defied the very laws of gravity.

The couple met in 1909, in St. Petersburg. They were both Jewish and from Vitebsk, in what is now Belarus, but from very different backgrounds. His father worked as a clerk in a herring warehouse; her family were wealthy jewelers. Both would recall their instant attraction.

In 1915, Marc and Bella married, and a year later had their only child, Ida. Following the Russian Revolution of 1917, Marc became Fine Arts Commissar for Vitebsk, a job he relished until being accused of promoting bourgeois individualism. The family moved to Moscow, where Marc found work designing theatrical sets. By now, they were disillusioned with the Soviet state and, in 1922, left Russia forever.

The rest of the 1920s and most of the 1930s were productive, happy years for the couple, who mainly lived in Paris, but their position became dangerous with the fall of France in World War II. In 1941, supporters smuggled them to America. They settled in New York City, where Bella completed a remarkable memoir of growing up in the Hasidic Jewish community of Vitebsk.

The liberation of Paris in August 1944 raised the prospect of returning to France. Tragically, Bella did not make it. That same month, she was taken to the hospital with a throat infection while on a holiday

Marc and Bella, 1926

in upstate New York. Due to wartime shortages, the hospital had no antibiotics, and she died. Distraught, Marc was unable to paint for months. Eventually, he returned to France, where he had a relationship with an Englishwoman, Virginia Haggard, and later with Valentina (Vava) Brodsky, a fellow Russian. Bella continued to haunt his art, though. When he died in 1985, at the age of 97, he had outlived her by more than 40 years.

> " Her silence is mine, her eyes mine.
> It is as if she knows everything about
> my childhood, my present, my future,
> as if she can see right through me. "

Marc Chagall, 1923

Georgia O'Keeffe

·——————·

Alfred Stieglitz

Artists unite

1916–1946

" My body is simply
crazy with wanting you **"**

Georgia O'Keeffe, 1929

A portrait of O'Keeffe by Stieglitz, 1920

Alfred Stieglitz was introduced to Georgia O'Keeffe in 1916, when he opened a tube stuffed with abstract charcoal drawings. Alfred, 52 years old and married, was an innovative photographer and a promoter of modern art in New York City. Georgia was 28 and single, an obscure art teacher living in South Carolina.

Without Georgia's permission, Alfred exhibited the drawings in his trailblazing 291 gallery. Georgia traveled to New York to express her anger, but Alfred placated her and shortly after this they began to correspond. In 1918, Alfred left his wife for Georgia.

The pair married in 1924 and remained so until Alfred's death in 1946, though Georgia craved more solitude than his hectic milieu provided. From 1929, she took many trips to New Mexico where the spareness made her feel "very tall inside and very still," but she always returned to Alfred. Her feelings about his place in her life are best expressed in her 1927 painting of the New York skyline, in which a skyscraper's red neon sign beams "ALFRED STIEGLITZ."

Valentine Ackland

◆

Sylvia Townsend Warner

The poet and the novelist

1930–1969

East Chaldon, Dorset, was the English village setting for the opening act of the mostly happy, 39-year same-sex partnership of the writers Sylvia Townsend Warner and Valentine Ackland. The relationship began when Sylvia renovated The Late Miss Green's Cottage, the official name of a property that she bought in the village in 1930, and asked Valentine to serve as its caretaker. Even today, the pair are together in East Chaldon, their ashes buried under the same gravestone behind the 14th-century church.

Sylvia was 34 when she met Valentine and already a successful novelist—*Lolly Willowes*, her pastoral fantasy of a spinster who moves to a hamlet named Great Mop and abandons her family for a relationship with the devil, had been published to acclaim and was even the first selection of the new Book of the Month Club, a subscription book service launched in the US. Valentine, who was 13 years younger than Sylvia, had fled a disastrous early marriage. Once she was living on her own, she began to live more androgynously, changing her given name to Valentine, cropping her golden hair into an Eton bob, and wearing men's trousers. She was a poet of quiet skill, but also had an instinct for the dramatic gesture—being a crack shot and, in Sylvia's words, driving with "a suavity ... like the

bowing of a master violinist." Sylvia described their partnership as "an unsurmised love, an irrefutable happiness" and their lives "joined up imperceptibly, along all their lengths."

The relationship endured, despite Valentine's excessive drinking and her affair with an American woman, Elizabeth Wade White, who stayed with the women in 1938. The wry, self-possessed Sylvia provided the steady, stable love that the more volatile Valentine craved. After Valentine's death from breast cancer in 1969, Sylvia wrote sporadically until her own death in 1978, always missing Valentine.

> ❝ My love for you is a terrible thing—as I warned you when I first told you I loved you. ❞
>
> **Valentine Ackland**, 1931

Frida Kahlo

Diego Rivera

The elephant and the dove

1928–1954

Frida Kahlo first saw Diego Rivera when she was 15 and he was painting a mural at her high school in Mexico City. She asked the renowned artist, 20 years her senior, if she could watch him work and spent the evening transfixed, her eyes following his every brushstroke. In another part of the room, Diego's wife looked on jealously, because her husband was a notorious womanizer. Diego later said that he had no idea that the petite schoolgirl would later be his wife. Frida, however, confided in a friend that she wanted to marry Diego and bear his children. This first encounter was their marriage in miniature: art, jealousy, passion, the dream of children. Between their first meeting and their second, Frida's life changed completely.

When Frida was 18, the bus she was riding in hit a tram, leaving her with dreadful injuries. She spent the next few months recovering. To pass the long, bedridden hours, she began to paint. Her subject was herself and her shattered body, a theme she would return to time and again, for she never fully recovered from the accident and went on to have more than 30 operations in an attempt to repair the damage. Her dream of becoming a doctor was replaced by a determination to paint.

" I love you more than my own skin. "

Frida Kahlo, 1935

In the 1930s, fascism was on the rise in Europe, and in Mexico a movement called Mexicanidad sought to replace the culture of the Spanish colonizers with the indigenous culture of the Aztecs. Diego, whose murals drew on the Aztec tradition of wall painting, was a leading figure in this movement. He saw himself as a revolutionary and went to meetings of the Mexican Communist Party, which Frida joined when she was well enough. When the two met again, Frida was 21—a woman not a girl. Within a year, Diego had divorced his wife and, in 1929, Frida and Diego married. Her parents called them the elephant and the dove due to their difference in size.

The newlyweds moved to the leafy city of Cuernavaca where they lived for love and art, painting without the distractions of Mexico City. Frida refined her vision, developing the Mexican style that would make her one of the most famous artists of the 20th century. She also forged her own highly recognizable personal style, wearing the loose embroidered blouses of her Mexican mother's Tehuana culture as well as long skirts, crowns of flowers, and chunky necklaces and rings. An icon was born.

In the early 1930s, Diego's work took them to San Francisco, Detroit, and New York City. They were a celebrity couple, the darlings of the art world. Frida became pregnant but due to damage to her womb caused by the accident, she had a miscarriage. It was the first of many failed pregnancies. At some point after this, Diego resumed his philandering ways. Frida claimed that she accepted his infidelities and that they were separate from their marriage. But when, on their return to Mexico, he began an affair with her younger sister Cristina, it crushed her. The pair began living separate lives, and Frida started taking lovers, too.

Diego easily accepted Frida's female lovers but was intensely jealous of the men she slept with. Divorce followed in 1939, but it did not end their passionate love story. Frida became gravely ill and Diego, then living in San Francisco, sent for her in order to get her better medical care. Their love reignited and they remarried on his 54th birthday in 1940. In her diary, Frida said, "The remarriage is working out well. Few quarrels, greater mutual understanding." Yet they were no more faithful. On their return to Mexico, they moved to the Casa Azul, Frida's childhood home on the outskirts of Mexico City. The marriage remained tempestuous, with both of them taking lovers, and Frida taunting Diego with her affairs, which included one with the Russian revolutionary Leon Trotsky.

Their marriage ended only with Frida Kahlo's death, reportedly from a pulmonary embolism, in 1954, at age 47—just a few days short of their 25th wedding anniversary. In his biography, Diego said of the time after her death: "Too late now I realized that the most wonderful part of my life had been my love for Frida" and wistfully recalled her tenderness and kindness.

Diego on my mind

Kahlo turned her suffering into art. Of her 150 paintings, 65 are self-portraits. They reveal in intimate and unflinching detail the physical torment caused by the tram accident that crippled her when she was in her late teens, as well as her miscarriages and the mental anguish caused by Rivera's many affairs. Some of the self-portraits include an image of Rivera on her forehead, a kind of mystical third eye, someone who was quite literally on her mind. She sometimes painted Diego with a third eye on his own forehead, a symbol of inner vision.

Frida Kahlo and Diego Rivera with their pet monkey c. 1945

> " There have been two great accidents in my life. One was the trolley, and the other was Diego. Diego was by far the worst. "

Frida Kahlo

Lillian Foster
❤
Mabel Hampton

The love birds of Harlem

1932–1978

Mabel Hampton and Lillian Foster's 46-year relationship began in Harlem, New York, in 1932 while waiting for the bus. Mabel had been a dancer and singer during the heyday of the Harlem Renaissance (1918 to the mid-1930s), when Harlem became the epicenter of a Black cultural explosion. Lillian worked in dry-cleaning establishments and was known for being a fashionable femme in New York's Black lesbian scene. Mabel preferred to wear men's suits, marking them as a visible lesbian couple when they were out together.

The love between Mabel and Lillian lasted until Lillian's death in 1978. They referred to each other as husband and wife and shared various apartments in Harlem before moving to a fourth-floor apartment in the Bronx in 1943, where they lived for the remainder of Lillian's life. Mabel was a prominent activist for gay and lesbian rights, helping cofound New York's Lesbian Herstory Archives in 1974, and serving as grand marshal of the New York City Gay and Lesbian Pride March in 1985, four years before her own death from pneumonia.

Benjamin Britten

— ◊ —

Peter Pears

Beloved men
1939–1976

For British composer Benjamin Britten and tenor Peter Pears, music was the very food of love. Soon after they met, Benjamin composed a part for Peter, the first of dozens he would write for the gifted young singer's golden voice. What began as friendship turned to a love that would last the rest of their lives after the men made a two-week crossing of the Atlantic Ocean together in 1939.

Benjamin's composition, *Seven Sonnets*, a setting of Michelangelo's poems to his male lover, is an ode to their love. Sung in Italian, the passionate yearning of one man for another may not have been evident to the London audience at the work's 1942 premiere. There was no translation in the program notes: at that time, and until 1967, sex between men was illegal in Britain.

To the outside world, Benjamin Britten and Peter Pears were an inseparable partnership of composer and singer; at home in the English seaside town of Aldeburgh, they were each other's beloved. In Benjamin's 1947 work *Canticle I*, Peter sings, "I my best beloved's am—so he is mine."

Near the end of their lives together, while Peter was in New York singing the lead role in Benjamin's last opera, *Death in Venice*, Benjamin wrote, "You are the greatest artist that ever was," to which Peter replied, "It is you who have given me everything ... I live in your music." Benjamin died in 1976 and Peter ten years later. They lie side by side beneath matching headstones in Aldeburgh's tiny cemetery.

Lauren Bacall

Humphrey Bogart

A Hollywood romance

1944–1957

❝ No one has ever written a romance better than we lived it. **❞**

Lauren Bacall, 2005

Shared laughter on the set of a TV remake of *The Petrified Forest* in 1955

S he was born Betty Perske in the Bronx and the world knew her as Lauren Bacall, but to the only man she ever loved—Humphrey Bogart—she was "Baby." He was kind, gentle, and vulnerable, a far cry from the hard-bitten heroes he played.

When Bacall, just 19 years old and in her first starring role, met screen legend Bogart on set, she shook with nerves. He put her at ease with his banter, and they developed an on-screen chemistry that eventually turned to real-life romance. Her mother disapproved of her dating a married man 25 years her senior, but no one could keep them apart.

After Bogart divorced his wife, the couple married, had two children, and starred in another three movies together before tragedy struck. Bogart was diagnosed with esophageal cancer, which would kill him in 1957. Bacall survived him by 57 years but wrote that her 12 years with Bogie were the happiest of her life.

Eva Perón

Juan Perón

A nation's darlings

1945–1972

" I have one thing that counts,
and that is my heart; it burns in
my soul, it aches in my flesh, and
it ignites my nerves; that is my
love for the people and Perón. "

Eva Perón, 1951

Juan Domingo Perón first met Eva "Evita" Duarte in Buenos Aires in 1944, while raising funds for the victims of a devastating earthquake. Juan was a 48-year-old politician and widower, and Eva a radio actress half his age. Eva, who had volunteered to collect donations, surprised him with her passion for helping those in need.

After meeting again at a charity gala, the couple began an intense relationship. Juan helped Eva develop a film career and she helped him increase his support among the working classes, propelling him to success. When he was imprisoned by political rivals in October 1945, an eruption of popular protest led to his swift release. The couple celebrated their union and the people's support by quietly marrying a few days later.

With the people on their side, Juan became president in 1946. As First Lady, Eva worked tirelessly to improve the lives of women and the poor—even when she began to show signs of illness. By the time the Peróns discovered she had cancer, it was too late for effective treatment. On July 26, 1952, Eva died at just 33. Her unexpected death devastated Juan and the people of Argentina.

Eva Perón and Juan Perón (right), 1951

Jackie Robinson

—◇—

Rachel Robinson

The dream team

1940–1972

In 1946, as Jackie Robinson, the man who would soon break the color barrier in Major League Baseball in the US, and his wife Rachel prepared to board a flight from Los Angles to Florida for spring training, Jackie's mother presented the newlyweds with a shoebox of fried chicken. In that era, Black Americans typically packed a lunch when traveling on trains and buses in the racially segregated South. Embarrassed, the stylish young couple reluctantly accepted the gift.

Several hours later, during a stopover in New Orleans, they were bumped from two flights, confronted with segregated restrooms, and refused seating in the airport restaurant. Exhausted and humiliated, they eventually found a room at a shabby hotel, and dug into the box Jackie's mother had packed, a bittersweet meal that strengthened their bond. The day's events foreshadowed the harassment and racism they would experience as Jackie made history on the baseball field.

Jackie and Rachel met at the University of California, Los Angeles (UCLA), in 1940, when he was a senior and a star athlete and she was a freshman studying nursing. They were shy but immediately drawn to each other. After Jackie served in the Army and Rachel graduated, they married within weeks of Jackie signing with the white leagues. For many years, Rachel ceded her nursing career to raising their three children and making their Stamford,

Jackie and Rachel, 1954

Connecticut, home a refuge for Jackie to escape the pressures of excelling on the field while simultaneously experiencing racial abuse. When he traveled, he wrote Rachel passionate letters expressing his love and gratitude.

Jackie left an impressive record when he retired in 1956, and in 1962 he was inducted in the National Baseball Hall of Fame. He and Rachel became outspoken advocates for civil rights. She enrolled at New York University and earned a master's degree in psychiatric nursing. On an October morning in 1972, while dressing for a doctor's appointment, Jackie suddenly ran toward Rachel and embraced her, declared his love, and dropped dead from a heart attack. He was 53.

> " My life when you are near is the closest to heaven I have ever been. "

Jackie Robinson, 1947

Julia Child

◈

Paul Child

Bon appétit!

1946–1994

Cookbook writer Julia Child met husband Paul during World War II, when they were both working for the Office of Strategic Services, a US intelligence agency, in Ceylon (now Sri Lanka). Julia, then Julia McWilliams, was 31 and a self-described social butterfly; Paul, ten years older, was quiet and artistic. They became friends, fell in love, and married in the US in 1946. They shared a love of fun and food, which would shape their lives.

After the war, the pair moved to Paris, where Paul worked for the US Information Service. On their first day in France, they drove from the port to Paris, stopping for lunch at France's oldest restaurant, La Couronne in Rouen. It was Julia's first experience of French food and the most exciting meal of her life. Paul ordered oysters, sole meunière in brown butter, green salad, and a crisp white wine, followed by a creamy soft cheese, and finishing with inky coffee. It was simple and elegant, each bite a revelation to Julia.

When she married, Julia couldn't cook and the first dinner she made, brains in red wine, was an unappetizing mess. Other dining disasters followed, which Paul, a connoisseur of good food and fine wine, ate without a word of criticism. When she arrived in France, Julia knew nothing about French food and couldn't speak the language. A few years later, she spoke fluent French, had a diploma from Le Cordon Bleu, France's most prestigious cooking school, and had started writing *Mastering the Art of French Cooking,* her life's work and the definitive work on French cooking in English.

> " We had a happy marriage because we were together all the time. "

Julia Child

In 1961, the Childs returned to the US. With the success of her book that year, and a TV series in 1963, Julia took center stage and Paul became the behind-the-scenes fixer. They traveled together, promoting her books and TV shows, Paul using his practical abilities to aid his wife—building a kitchen suited to her 6 ft 2 in (1.88 meter) height— and Julia involving him in everything. They saw themselves almost as one person, signing letters PJ, or Pulia. Rather than Christmas cards, they sent Valentine's cards to friends including one of them in a bubble bath mischievously saying, "Wish you were here." In 1994, after a long decline, Paul died, leaving Julia to continue her work alone, bolstered by her memories of their shared love and laughter.

Ossie Davis

Ruby Dee

Actors and activists

Together for 59 years, actors Ruby Dee and Ossie Davis helped shape Black American culture and transform Black civil rights. United by a love of the theater and a passion for activism, they used their craft to portray the Black experience and supported leading figures in the civil rights movement.

Ruby, who grew up in New York City, joined Harlem's American Negro Theater (ANT) while studying modern languages at Hunter College in 1940. Ossie, an aspiring playwright from Georgia, had traveled to New York to gain some acting experience on the advice of his professor at Howard University, in Washington, D.C. Attracted to the culture and atmosphere of Harlem, he joined the Rose McClendon Players, another Black theater group.

Ossie and Ruby were thrown together in 1946 when they secured the leading roles in Robert Ardrey's play *Jeb* on Broadway. Ruby didn't like Ossie at first, finding him "peculiar." However, while watching him rehearse, she suddenly felt a strong connection. Their Broadway debut was short-lived—running for only nine performances—but *Jeb* proved to be the first of many collaborations.

In 1946, Ruby and Ossie found themselves working together in *Anna Lucasta*, the first Broadway play with an all-Black cast. While still friends, the pair grew closer when the play went on tour, and after

> " As I watched him, I felt something like a bolt of lightning ... I'd never felt anything like that before. "

Ruby Dee, 1998

Ruby left the production to star in a film, Ossie found her waiting for him at the station when he returned to New York. On December 9, 1948—a rare day off for them—the pair traveled to New Jersey and found a priest to marry them, with Ruby's sister and Ossie's brother as witnesses. From then on, Ruby and Ossie became a power couple—both on and off the stage.

After their first child was born in 1952, Ruby returned to her acting career, despite the expectations for married women and mothers at the time. Ossie gave his wife his full support and often stayed home with the children. The couple continued to perform in various plays together, including Lorraine Hansberry's *A Raisin in the Sun* (1959)—the first play by a Black American woman on Broadway.

Ruby and Ossie also found success together on the small and silver screens. In 1961, Ossie realized his ambitions as a writer, when his play *Purlie Victorious*, a satire on racism, appeared on Broadway with Ruby and him in the leading roles. Later in life, Ossie and Ruby agreed that the play was a career highlight for them both—a treasured collaboration that started in their family home. The show's success also led to the couple meeting militant civil rights activist Malcolm X, who would become a dear friend.

Throughout their lives, Ossie and Ruby were prominent political campaigners. The theater scene of 1940s Harlem, where they first met, was a crucible for the fight against racial intolerance. Weeks before Malcolm X was assassinated in February 1965, Ruby helped draw up plans for a meeting between Malcolm X and the more moderate Martin Luther King, Jr., hoping that they would see past their differences and realize their common goal. Despite the risks posed by their political campaigning—to their lives as well as their careers—the couple continued their fight for racial justice.

Alongside their political campaigning, Ruby and Ossie's careers continued to thrive. In 1989, a new generation was introduced to the couple by Black film director Spike Lee's *Do the Right Thing*. In 1998, the couple celebrated their 50th wedding anniversary and commemorated the occasion with the publication of a joint autobiography, *With Ossie and Ruby: In This Life Together*. Their shared lifetime contribution to American culture was recognized in 2004, when they received the Kennedy Center Honors award.

Ossie died in 2005. Before her own death in 2014, Ruby spoke of her hope to be reunited with her husband: "At 90, I've had time to realize there's really no such thing as death. When I'm reincarnated, I hope Ossie and I continue the journey together."

An open marriage

When Ruby and Ossie published their autobiography in 1998, readers were surprised to discover that the couple initially had an open marriage. Described as an experiment by the pair, they agreed they could sleep with other people, as long as they were honest with one another and discreet, and did not expose the family or the other party to harm. Although the couple soon realized that they only wanted each other, they remembered those early years as a freeing experience that gave them a new understanding of love and marriage.

We were in love, head
over heels, and stuck with
each other forever!

Ossie Davis, 1998

Ossie and Ruby, 1998

Paul Newman

Joanne Woodward

Lust and respect

1957–2008

The marriage of Joanne Woodward, Oscar-winning star of *The Three Faces of Eve* (1957), and legendary, blue-eyed leading man Paul Newman, of *The Sting* (1973) and numerous other box office hits, lasted 50 years, from their wedding in 1958 to his death in 2008, defying the pattern of most Hollywood relationships.

The pair met in 1953 on Broadway, where 28-year-old Paul, a World War II US Navy veteran, had been cast as the leading man in *Picnic* by William Inge, while Joanne, a Southern belle from Georgia, was an understudy in the play. Paul was already married to Jackie Witte, who had sacrificed her own acting career to raise their children.

The two stars both felt the pull of attraction but did not act on it, and Paul had a third child with Jackie in 1954. Things changed when Paul landed the role of boxer Rocky Graziano in *Somebody Up There Likes Me* (1956) and saw more of Joanne in Hollywood. In 1957, the pair were cast together in *The Long, Hot Summer*, shot in Louisiana. The romance flourished on location, and by the time shooting finished, Joanne was pregnant.

Jackie, betrayed and angry, initially refused to divorce Paul. Eventually, she relented, and Joanne and Paul married in January 1958. The years to come would bring tragedies, notably the death from an overdose of Scott, Paul and Jackie's eldest child, but the marriage between him and Joanne lasted, producing three daughters. There were rumors of infidelities by Paul, but the overwhelming testimony of their friends is of a demonstrative passion that never faded.

Chinua Achebe

◇

Christie Okoli–Achebe

Lucky in love
1961–2013

When Christie Chinwe Okoli first met Chinua Achebe, author of *Things Fall Apart*, at the Nigerian Broadcasting Service in 1958, she thought to herself, "This man's wife is very lucky." But he was unmarried, and love blossomed between the pair. In 1961, they wed.

The future would bring extreme adversity. In 1966, violence erupted in Nigeria and thousands of Igbo people were massacred by their neighbours. The Achebes, who were Igbos, fled Lagos. Eastern Nigeria broke away to become Biafra, and a civil war followed. Chinua, the new country's most famous son, traveled the world seeking money and support, while Christie and their children stayed behind, often under attack. After Biafra's defeat in 1970, the family moved to the US.

Now it was Christie's time. She studied for a doctorate while her husband, a professor at the University of Massachusetts, took over at home. In 1990, a car accident in Nigeria left Chinua partially paralyzed. "Christie saved me," he said of his rehabilitation. The father of African literature died in 2013 and was laid to rest in his hometown in Nigeria.

Johnny Cash

◊

June Carter Cash

Love's extremes

1968–2003

During their 35 years of marriage, singers June Carter and Johnny Cash tested their love for each other to the limits. When they first met in Nashville in 1955, Johnny had recently married his longtime sweetheart Vivian Liberto. June was also married, to honky-tonk singer Carl Smith. The Arkansas-born Johnny was at the start of his musical career, following four years' service with the US Air Force. June, from a well-known Country music dynasty headed by her mother, Maybelle Carter, had been performing since the age of ten.

That first encounter was fleeting, but it made a deep impression on both of them. Johnny, familiar with June's work, declared that he had always wanted to meet her; she felt that she knew him already.

In 1956, Johnny released the song that was to become his first major hit, "I Walk the Line." By this time, Elvis Presley was a fan, and, without realizing it, helped stoke the romance between June and Johnny. June often accompanied Presley to concerts, after which he would take her to bars and make her listen to Johnny's songs on the jukebox.

By the 1960s, Johnny's career had taken off, and by now June regularly accompanied him on tour, singing backup and duets. There was no escaping the intense attraction between them, yet neither felt

> " I can't fall in love with this man,
> but it's just like a ring of fire. "

June Carter Cash, 2000

easy about their feelings for each other. It was not just that both were already married—he to Vivian, she to a second husband by then, former football player Edwin ("Rip") Nix—but also that June was only too aware of Johnny's wild and self-destructive lifestyle, with its intense touring schedules fueled by alcohol, amphetamine, and barbiturate addictions.

Johnny's 1963 hit, "Ring of Fire," cowritten by June (with fellow singer Merle Kilgore), echoes this anxiety. June would later tell the story of the song's creation—how, restless and unable to sleep one night, she was out driving her car as fast as she could when she became acutely aware of the situation she found herself in. It was like a ring of fire, she said. She both loved Johnny and did not want to love him. As she put it on another occasion, falling in love with Johnny was one of the most painful things that ever happened to her.

In the end, the force of love proved irresistible. They divorced their spouses in 1966, and two years later, when they were both in their late thirties Johnny finally overcame June's resistance to marriage when he proposed to her in front of a live audience in Canada. They married just over a week later in Kentucky, and their son John Carter Cash was born in 1970—June already had two daughters by her previous marriages and Johnny four daughters with Vivian.

Marriage did not necessarily bring tranquility. For Johnny, with his addictions, there was a pattern of rehabilitation, a few years' abstinence, followed by relapse, with his last stint in rehab in 1991. June did her best to save her husband from himself, including by flushing his drugs down the toilet. But she had issues of her own. According to their son John, she was a compulsive shopper with an addiction to prescription pills, and her extravagance brought her and Johnny close to financial disaster in the 1980s. Nor was Johnny entirely faithful to her. Even so, the love between them endured, June giving Johnny what he was the first to describe as unconditional love. He knew and freely acknowledged that he owed his life to her.

On May 15, 2003, June died of complications following heart surgery. On July 5, in what turned out to be his last public performance, Johnny, who was a man of deep Christian faith despite his often wild lifestyle, read out a statement in which he spoke of the spirit of June overshadowing him with the love she had for him and the love he had for her. He felt, he said, as if she was visiting him that night from heaven, giving him courage and inspiration "like she always has."

Johnny died on September 12, 2003, just short of four months after her death, of complications related to diabetes. He had kept on working until near the end, recording the vocals for his last two albums, which were released posthumously. It was Johnny's way of dealing with heartbreak.

A public proposal

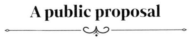

On February 22, 1968, Johnny Cash proposed to June in front of a capacity audience of 7,000 people in London, Ontario. They had just completed the song "Jackson," containing the line "We got married in a fever" when Johnny, keeping hold of his microphone, turned to June and asked her to be his wife. An astonished and embarrassed June could only reply, "Sing another." But Johnny insisted, "Not till you answer me." June begged the band, "Play another," but Johnny persisted, and eventually she said, "Yes." She later said she would have liked him to get down on one knee but "that's not the way it was."

June and Johnny, 1969

" When it gets dark and everybody's gone home and the lights are turned off, it's just me and her. "

Johnny Cash, 2000

Cookie Johnson

◇

Magic Johnson

Love conquers all

1977–today

" Marrying her is
the smartest thing
I've ever done. "

Magic Johnson, 1991

Cookie and Magic, 2019

On November 7, 1991, one of the world's most famous professional basketball stars, Earvin "Magic" Johnson, announced his retirement from the Los Angeles Lakers. He was only 32, but he had recently learned he was HIV positive, then thought to be a death sentence. Behind him sat his pregnant wife of five weeks, Earleatha "Cookie" Johnson.

Magic and Cookie had been dating since college, but Magic had not always been faithful to her, and had contracted HIV through unsafe sex with other women. His decision to disclose his HIV status helped dispel stigma against the virus and combat the myth that it only affected gay men.

Despite his infidelity, Cookie did not leave Magic. Strengthened by her religious faith, she resolved to help him live. Except for a two-week separation in 2001, the couple has stuck together, advocating on behalf of people with HIV, starting new businesses, and supporting their two children. Magic even played some more basketball. The road was not always smooth, but love conquered all. In this marriage, Cookie is the point guard—and for her, their team comes first.

David Bowie

◇

Iman

The stars align

1992–2016

They were two of the highest profile people in the world—Somalian supermodel Iman and innovative British singer-songwriter David Bowie—yet the hallmarks of their nearly 24 years of marriage were privacy, stability, and a quiet day-to-day domesticity.

The pair met in 1990 at a dinner party organized by Iman's hairdresser. The 43-year-old Bowie had in the past variously described himself as gay, bisexual, and a "closet heterosexual." He had been married to model and actress Angie Barnett, with whom he had his son Duncan. Iman, twice married and with a daughter, Zulekha, was 35—the imposing beauty who had inspired Gianni Versace, Donna Karan, Yves St. Laurent, and Calvin Klein.

Bowie lost no time in wooing the initially more reserved Iman, inviting her for afternoon tea and meeting her off a flight from Paris with an armful of flowers. They made their first public appearance together in December 1990 and married in Lausanne, Switzerland, in April 1992. Their daughter Alexandria was born in 2000.

Iman would say later that she fell in love with David Jones (Bowie's birth name), not Bowie, the public persona. Their privacy was crucial, especially when David was diagnosed with liver cancer. David made his last public appearance at the opening of his off-Broadway musical, *Lazarus*, in December 2015. His 25th album, *Blackstar*, was released on January 8, 2016, two days before he died. In later years, when someone referred to Bowie as Iman's "late" husband, she objected—David, she said, was still, and always would be, her husband.

David and Iman, 2003

" That she would be my wife,
in my head was a done deal ...
I just knew she was the one. "

David Bowie, 2000

Barack Obama

◇

Michelle Robinson Obama

Double firsts

1991–present

❝ Any worries I'd been harboring about my life and career and even about Barack himself seemed to fall away with that first kiss. ❞

Michelle Obama, 2018

Michelle and Barack Obama, 2009

When Michelle Robinson was working at a Chicago law firm in 1989, she was asked to mentor a law student. Her mentee, Barack Obama, was said to be smart and attractive by some of her colleagues, and just two years older than her. When Barack started asking her out on dates, she refused multiple times, not wishing to compromise her professional integrity. It was only when he offered to leave the law firm that she agreed to go for ice cream. They shared their first kiss on the curb outside Baskin-Robbins.

This simple beginning eventually led to marriage in 1992 and the birth of daughters Malia and Sasha in 1998 and 2001. In 2004, Barack would become a US senator, and four years later, the 44th President of the United States—the country's first Black president. Michelle, as First Lady, was warm and relatable, and became a witty champion of the global rights of girls and women. As they both admit in their autobiographies, the stresses of politics put their marriage under enormous strain, but their relationship ultimately survived, anchored by love, friendship, and mutual respect.

Index

Acknowledgments

Toucan Books

Editorial Director Ellen Dupont; **Editor** Dorothy Stannard; **Designer** Dave Jones; **Picture Researcher** Sharon Southren; **Researcher** Benjamin Hartnell-Booth; **Sensitivity Readers** Sue George, Kit Heyam, Pas Paschali, Brian Robinson; **Proofreader** Julie Brooke; **Indexer** Marie Lorimer

Authors

Elizabeth Barrington, Elizabeth Blakemore, Mary Frances Budzik, Mark Collins Jenkins, Jacob Field, Andrew Kerr-Jarrett, Ethan Segal, Marian Smith Holmes, Deborah Soden, Shannon Weber